CONTENTS

Foreword 5

In the Beginning 7

My Own Freewill 13

To Tithe or Not to Tithe 23

Real Sacrifices 39

First Things First 47

Seedtime and Harvest 55

The Principles of Stewardship 65

The Law of Exchange 79

Money is the Solution 91

A Place for Money 97

Acknowledgements 105

About the Author 107

Foreword

As a citizen of God's kingdom, your life must be aligned with His principles. This book highlights the principles governing the economy of God, principles which operate similar to the laws governing the natural economy.

If you've ever wondered what the word of God has to say about giving, this book will prove to be an invaluable resource. In the pages of this book, Dr. Hearns provides the biblical basis for offerings such as tithing, freewill, sacrifices, and first fruits. Moreover, he reveals spiritual aspects of giving many churches today aren't teaching.

Just as natural laws govern the world's economy, spiritual principles govern the economy of God's kingdom. They can be difficult to recognize because of spiritual ignorance or stubbornness. However, whether you acknowledge them or pass the consequences of your failure to adhere to them off as bad luck or coincidence, you have still felt the effects of these principles in your life. Just as gravity does not need your approval to operate, the principles of God's kingdom work whether you observe them or not.

As a child of God, you will discover your life runs smoother when governed by kingdom principles. As you explore the principles outlined in this book and incorporate them into your life, you will find they are just as relevant and effective today as they were thousands of years ago. As you read this book, I pray you will allow the Holy Spirit to speak to you about God's plan for the finances He has allowed you to manage for Him.

Bishop Brandon B Porter
Prelate of Central Tennessee Jurisdiction
General Board Member
Church of God in Christ International

In the Beginning

Man was created to worship. Giving has always been an integral part of the worship experience. If you will observe the first family of the Bible, you will be able to glean some valuable lessons on giving from their examples.

> And Adam knew Eve his wife; and she conceived, and bare Cain, and said, I have gotten a man from the LORD. And she again bare his brother Abel. And Abel was a keeper of sheep, but Cain was a tiller of the ground. And in process of time it came to pass, that Cain brought of the fruit of the ground an offering unto the LORD. And Abel, he also brought of the firstlings of his flock and of the fat thereof. And the LORD had respect unto Abel and to his offering: but unto Cain and to his offering he had not respect. Genesis 4:1-5

In the first verse Eve acknowledges that the Lord gave her a son ("I have gotten a man from the LORD"). A vital part of worship is acknowledging God as the source of all things. When you recognize God as your source, you have no problem giving to Him. You realize all things come from Him.

This is one of the differences between the true and living God and the pagan gods worshipped by the heathen. The heathen in their worship thought it was necessary to give sacrifices to appease their gods. Often these pagan gods were demonically inspired and demanded sacrifices of children. There are several occasions recorded in scripture where the people caused their children to pass through the fire when sacrificing to these bloodthirsty idols.

As Cain and Abel grew older, they were found participating in worship. Although the Bible is not specific on the type of offerings they gave, some aspects of this offering reflect the tithe, others the first fruit offering, and still others the sacrifice offering. All these offerings can be summed up in one word: worship.

When you realize giving is an integral part of worship, you no longer need someone to tell you how often to give or to demand a specific amount. By examining their offering more closely, one realizes these two brothers exemplify two distinct paths to giving. Abel is demonstrating Spirit-led giving, and Cain is being led by his flesh.

At first glance, you might think there isn't much difference in the way they bring their offerings to the Lord. They both make freewill offerings. To the best of my knowledge, there is no law at this point concerning giving or a priesthood to encourage it, yet they bring an offering to God. However, upon closer observation, there are noted differences between their styles of giving.

Abel is a shepherd. When he gives his offering to the Lord, he gives of the firstling of his flock. Cain, on the other hand, is a tiller of the ground. He brings fruit of the ground to the Lord. Again, this seems comparable. Each offered the fruit of his labor to the Lord.

Scripture says "in the process of time" Cain brought of the fruit of the ground. Let's examine these words in the original Hebrew to see what is really being said about Cain's offering. According to Strong's Concordance, the word "process" is derived from the Hebrew word (qets) which literally means end of a space of time (H7093). The word "time" here comes from the Hebrew word (yowm), meaning a day or period (H3117). By referencing the original Hebrew, we see Cain's offering was made at the end of the allotted time, or perhaps the end of the harvest season. In this respect, Cain's offering was not a first fruit offering, and probably not given in the same spirit as Abel's.

What could possibly be so important to Cain that he put the things of God on the back burner? This question could be answered in one word: life. Life can become extremely complicated and demanding. There are times you will desire to do something for God, but at the end of the day, all you have is the desire. To understand why Cain had such a hard time pleasing God with his offering, you must understand two other words. The first is sacrifice. Often when you think of sacrifice you think of the value of the object being offered. This is a large part of sacrifice. In this case, an argument could be made about the content of Cain's offering. Even though he brought the fruit of the ground, which is how he made his living, he could easily have purchased or bartered with his brother and brought a blood sacrifice to the Lord. The scripture says that without the shedding of blood there is no remission of sin (Hebrews 9:22).

Could this be the reason the Lord had no respect for Cain's offering? There's a lot to be said about this possibility, but I believe there is another to consider. Giving is an integral part of the Christian experience. God gave His Son, and His Son gave His life. In each instance, the giving involved sacrifice of the best thing available. In Cain's case, his offering consisted of the fruit he gave. Anything you could use for your own pleasure but choose to dedicate to the Lord is an offering, but it's not necessarily a sacrifice.

With this idea in mind, let's look at Cain's method of offering. Waiting until the end of the period allotted means God's offering was not a priority for Cain. In other words, he wasn't willing to sacrifice his time or agenda to give an offering to God. First fruits literally mean "to put God first." Giving of your first fruits says you are willing to put your agenda on the backburner and give God the preeminence He deserves in all things. By putting the things of God first, you are keeping your life in perspective. It is imperative in your walk with God that you realize you're not the center of the world.

You may be thinking this issue isn't important. Cain brought God an offering, and since there was no law, he did more than was required. However, careful examination of the scriptures will reveal that even though the law had not been instituted, Cain and Abel still had knowledge of what was required of them:

> And the LORD said unto Cain, Why art thou wroth? and why is thy countenance fallen? If thou doest well, shalt thou not be accepted? and if thou doest not well, sin lieth at the door. And unto thee shall be his desire, and thou shalt rule over him. Genesis 4:6-7

In these verses, God is dealing with Cain. God would not have mentioned doing well if there wasn't an established protocol Cain knew. The first thing God addresses is Cain's attitude. Cain is angry and feeling rejected. From his attitude, it is apparent he feels entitled to better treatment from God. He feels slighted.

Why does Cain feel this way? The most obvious reason is because he feels whatever he does should be accepted. This attitude of entitlement spits in the face of grace and causes people to feel like everyone, including God, owes them something. These qualities seem to be an integral part of Cain's character.

If you do an in-depth study of the book of Genesis, you will find Cain didn't acquire this attitude accidentally. It's possible these feelings were instilled in Cain by his mother. Look at the prophecy given to Eve in the third chapter of Genesis:

> and I will put enmity between thee and the woman, and between thy seed and her seed; it shall bruise thy head, and thou shalt bruise his heel. Genesis 3:15

It is easy to see why Eve would think Cain is the seed that would bruise the serpent's head. This is even more evident when you remember her words in Genesis 4:1:

> And Adam knew Eve his wife; and she conceived, and bare Cain, and said, I have gotten a man from the LORD.

The word used for man here is "Iysh (H376)." This word could be translated male, man or champion. The name Cain means possession or acquired. When she says, "I have gotten a man from the Lord," she disregards Adam's role in producing Cain and proclaims Cain is from the Lord. In other words, "the Lord has given me a champion to fulfill His prophecy." This no longer sounds like someone who is grateful for having been blessed with a child, but someone who feels vindicated because she has conceived a seed that will set everything right and reverse all the damage done by sin.

Whenever you feel as though you are the reason everything is wrong, you naturally want to be the one who is instrumental in fixing it. Although the promise was spoken to her and Adam, it would be forty-two generations in the making. By ignoring the spiritual implications of the promise, she could cause Cain to believe there is more to him than just the seed of Adam. This makes it easier to understand why Cain is not given to making deeper sacrifices to God. It's possible he has been raised to believe God needs him more than he needs God.

The offerings of Cain and Abel had qualities resembling most of the offerings listed in the Bible. The ones I will focus on in this book are the freewill offering, tithe, sacrifice, and first fruits. These concepts are supported and sustained by eternal principles in the word of God. These principles are the pillars undergirding the economy of God.

The concepts of freewill offerings, tithes, sacrifices, and first fruits overlap and encompass each other in many ways. Although I will endeavor to define each as a distinct activity, they can't be easily compartmentalized. It is virtually impossible to speak of each one separately.

My Own Freewill

The freewill offering, also known as an oblation, is mentioned several times in the Bible. The term suggests the offering is given willingly, without pressure by another party. When the Bible speaks about an oblation it is often referred to as prepared. This offering is generally dedicated to the Lord and is eaten by the priest. "And every oblation of thy meat offering shalt thou season with salt; neither shalt thou suffer the salt of the covenant of thy God to be lacking from thy meat offering: with all thine offerings thou shalt offer salt." Leviticus 2:13. The oblation represents an offering that has been prepared for the priest to eat. Since the priest were to live a life of service, they were not given an inheritance with the children of Israel, therefore they had to rely on the generosity of the other tribes for their sustenance.

The worshipper was instructed to offer this oblation with salt. The salt was used not only to enhance the flavor, but also as a preservative. In the case the salt is referred to as the salt of the covenant of thy god. Both qualities of salt have spiritual significance to the covenant of Israel. As a preservative the salt is a reminder of the eternal strength of the covenant that God has made with Israel. As seasoning the salt reflects the goodness of the Lord. "O taste and see that the LORD *is* good: blessed *is* the man *that* trusteth in him."

The idea of oblation has been a part of the worship experience since the beginning. Most churches agree with the term freewill offering and there is little dispute over whether one should receive a freewill offering. Most take the view receiving a freewill offering is not legalistic, as one has a choice whether to participate or not. In today's church, the freewill offering is usually given in money. Money is the approved means of transacting business in the world as well as the church. During the Old Testament age, they prepared the oblation from the animals they raised or acquired through business transactions. Today money is offered by those who have gained through business or labor.

The idea of freewill suggests two distinct characteristics of such an offering. First, there should be no stipulation on the amount one chooses to give. This means the worshipper should feel free to give whatever amount he or she chooses to give without being pressured by anyone to give a different amount. In today's church, when specific needs arise, the minister or finance official can petition the assembly for a more generous gift, but it is still up to the worshipper to decide how much he or she wants to give.

Second, the idea of freewill also implies the time the gift is offered is at the discretion of the one offering. Most worship services have an appointed time the offering is received, but it is up to the worshipper to decide if he or she wants to give at this time or wait until the next opportunity. The finance officer can solicit any amount at any time, but it is ultimately up to the worshipper to determine how much and how often he or she wants to give. Any other condition does not fit the description of freewill.

Some churches employ gimmicks and catchy sayings to entice worshippers to give more than they would ordinarily give. Although these techniques are sometimes effective, they reflect a lack of faith, and do nothing to effectively increase the faith of the believers. The best way of increasing the amount of the freewill offering is through teaching the natural and spiritual benefits of giving. No amount of pressure or gimmicks are a substitute for good teaching based on the word of God. When a worshipper understands the kingdom principles of seedtime and harvest, they are better able to see their gift for what it truly is, and they are more willing to give.

The term freewill is a compound word consisting of the words free and will. Both words imply an attitude that enhances one's ability to give. The word free simply means it is mine, so I can give without permission on my own authority. Although it cost me something it is offered freely as a gift. The word will mean this is not something that I am obligated to do. I give this because I want to give and it blesses my spirit to give it as an offering to the work of the ministry. Since this offering is given of my own free will, it is no the church's responsibility to dictate the terms of my giving.

Regrettably, many churches today are postured towards begging for money, rather than trusting God to meet their needs. It is impossible to teach faith if you don't have it. As a Pastor or church leader, your faith must be in God to meet your needs, not the people God sends to you. The more time you spend trusting God, the less time you will spend trying to trick and entice people to increase their offering to meet the needs of ministry.

There are eternal truths in the word of God one must implement if they want to see increases in the financial support of the ministry. When one recognizes and incorporates these truths, the natural consequences will include an increase in offerings to meet the needs of the ministry. Furthermore, by putting these truths into action, you will find your finances moving from natural to supernatural. The reason so many ministers don't incorporate these simple truths into their ministry is because they are either unaware that they exist, or they haven't grown to the level of faith necessary to trust God at His word.

The first truth you must learn is **God is your source.** "But my God shall supply all your need according to his riches in glory by Christ Jesus." Philippians 4:19. One merely needs to understand the power of these words to be delivered from the mentality of works. When you yoke your prosperity to your works, you will always be burdened by the cares of life and ministry. If you feel like you are the one who must make things happen, you allow no room for grace to operate in your life. The oblation was not a result of the priest's work; it was prepared by the worshippers and offered to the priest. Just as the oblation was presented to the priest in the Old Testament, grace is available to believers today.

In John 21, after the crucifixion the disciples encounter the resurrected Lord on the seashore. When he encounters them, they had returned to their old lifestyle. This is not as unusual as one might think. You must remember their whole world has been turned upside down. Although they were warned that Jesus would be taken away, they had never accepted that possibility. In their minds Jesus would always be with them supplying the answers and showing them the way. It was easy for them to see him as their source when he was among them multiplying the fish and the loaves. Their lives had been powerfully impacted by his presence, and now he was gone.

Life without him was something they could not have even imagined.

After an encounter with Jesus sometimes people still tend to return to what used to work for them. While Jesus was among them, they were excited about the transformation they were experiencing. Yet when he was gone, they felt a need to return to what worked best for them. This is when they realized that something had changed. Although they were expert fisherman, they had fished all night and caught nothing. Sunrise was confirmation that an entire night of fishing was in vain.

It is times like this that you don't want to see anybody. You just want to quietly disappear and drown in your own failure. It is also at times like these that Jesus shows up. When they encountered Jesus the thing that is so amazing is the fact that they did not recognize him for who he was. This could've been for several reasons, he obviously looked different because he was in his resurrected body. Also, the last time they would have seen him his body had been beaten beyond recognition. Add to this the fact that their faith really had not developed to the point where they expected to ever see him again, and their perception is veiled in failure and defeat. When he shows up, he asks them if they have any meat. This was probably the last thing they wanted to deal with. It is bad enough to have failed in the one thing you thought you were proficient at, but it's even worse when what appears to be a stranger rub it in your face by asking for the one thing that you don't have.

This had to be a humbling experience because they had toiled all night and yet there was nothing to show for their efforts. These were not ordinary men trying their hands at fishing; they made their living as professional fishermen. If anyone should have known how to catch fish, it was these men. Yet when confronted with the reality of their condition, they were forced to admit they had gained nothing from their effort. Reluctantly and painfully their answer was a resounding no.

Jesus instructed them to cast their nets on the right side of the boat. They could've accepted this as an insult. After a night of trying they could easily had said we have had enough. Scripture does not indicate that they knew it was Jesus, so there is no reason they should have felt obligated to do what he said. But these were desperate times and they called for desperate measures. Rather than go home empty handed to their families they were willing to try anything. After all what could it hurt. Especially since the alternative offered no consolation.

When they followed His instructions, they caught a multitude of fish. Even though their works had produced nothing, there was still grace available to exceed their needs. Jesus could have berated them for going back to their old lifestyle, but instead He showed them that it could work for them if they needed it to work. He gave them more than enough of what they were working for, yet when they made it to the shore, He showed them a more excellent way.

God's plan was not for them to go back to fishing, but He still showed them they could be blessed even as fishermen if they heeded the voice of the Lord. Just because something is working for you does not mean it's God's best for you. The important lesson here has nothing to do with fishing, but everything to do with hearing the voice of the Lord. By following simple instructions, they made up for a whole night's losses in one moment. Yet when they made it to the shore, they found something even more intriguing. No amount of fish could have prepared them for what they saw when they came to the seashore.

When these fishermen came to the seashore at the end of a frustrating night, there is Jesus cooking fish for them to eat. The fish were already prepared for them. This would've been representative of a type of oblation or freewill offering. The disciples, who represented the New Testament priesthood, were attempting to go back to their old ways of supporting themselves through their own efforts. They spent the whole night fishing and caught nothing. This shows the results of works versus grace. Your best efforts to produce something to sustain you outside of the will of God will not produce enough for your needs. This is true whether you are talking about fishing or working two jobs trying to make ends meet. Although their works produced nothing, grace prepared an oblation in the form of cooked fish. Like the oblations of old, the fish were prepared and offered freely with no effort on their behalf.

This was a prophetic act by Jesus. He was letting them know by preparing a simple meal, that he could supply their needs. Even after their haul of fish, there remained work to be done before they could eat. A fire had to be started, and the fish had to be cleaned and cooked. All this work was necessary before they could eat. By preparing them a meal, Jesus was saying to them "I have already made provisions for you. You no longer need to provide for yourself when you do My will. When you take care of My business, I'll take care of yours."

Like the fish prepared by Jesus for the disciples, the freewill offering is given willingly and prepared for those who serve in the ministry. But what happens when the people refuse to give the portions due to the priest and those who serve in the ministry? Old Testament scripture states the ramifications of being unwilling to support the ministry.

> And I perceived that the portions of the Levites had not been given *them:* for the Levites and the singers, that did the work, were fled every one to his field. Then contended I with the rulers, and said, Why is the house of God forsaken? And I gathered them together, and set them in their place. Then brought all Judah the tithe of the corn and the new wine and the oil unto the treasuries. Nehemiah 13:10-12

As Nehemiah was rebuilding the wall, he was also restoring the priesthood. Whenever the enemy attacks a ministry, one of the areas he focuses on is finances. One sure way of destabilizing a work is to convince the people not to support the ministry financially. When those appointed to serve in the ministry are forced to sustain themselves, the ministry suffers. Nehemiah perceived the Levites were not being given their allotted portions. Because of this they were forced to go into the fields to find ways to support themselves. This would take away from time better served in the temple. Whenever your minister must work a secular job, you are not getting his best. You might be getting good, but there is better available if the man of God is free to serve God on a full-time basis.

In Acts 6, the apostles recognized their service in the ministry could not be interrupted by settling issues between the widows. Therefore, they created the office of the deacon. It has always been the enemies' desire to separate the called from his or her calling. When worshippers refuse to participate fully in the freewill offering, the enemy's agenda is fulfilled.

The first thing that comes to most people's mind when they think of the freewill offering is the offering plate passed around on Sunday morning. Regardless of the denomination and the affiliation this offering is usually received. Because this offering is so regularly taken and most of the time without a long discourse, the worshipper usually gives little thought to the amount he or she gives. Other offerings are not so readily received in different denominations. One of the most controversial offerings in the Bible is the tithe. There remains more division in the church concerning the tithe than any other offering discussed in this book.

To Tithe or Not to Tithe

By far, no other offering is more hotly disputed than the tithe. Divisions persist in local congregations over the issue of tithing. Here are the findings of a recent survey among Evangelicals on tithing:

Survey: Minority of Evangelical Leaders Say Bible Requires Tithing

Thou shalt not be required to financially support your church – but you should anyway.

That's the upshot of a new informal survey of evangelical leaders finding that less than half believe that the Bible requires church members to tithe, the practice of giving at least 10 percent of one's income to the church. The survey, conducted by the National Association of Evangelicals (NAE) among its 100-member board of directors, found that 42% of evangelical leaders believe the Bible requires tithing, while 58% do not. "The Old Testament called for multiple tithes, sort of combining government taxes with religious stewardship," NAE President Leith Anderson said, reacting to the survey. "Since there is such a strong evangelical tradition of tithing, I was a little surprised that a majority of our evangelical leaders say the tithe system of the Old Testament does not carry over to the New Testament or to us," Anderson said in a statement.

The National Association of Evangelicals, the nation's biggest evangelical umbrella organization, would not say how many of its 100 board members responded to the survey, which was conducted in February. The board includes such influential figures as the heads of the Salvation Army, the Assemblies of God - a major Pentecostal denomination - and the National Hispanic Christian Leadership Conference.

The injunction to tithe comes from the Old Testament, or what Jews call the Hebrew Bible, which tells of Abraham and others giving ten percent of war spoils, a harvest or other goods as offerings to God or religious leaders. Dan Olson, a Purdue University sociology professor who has studied tithing, says the new survey doesn't mean Christian leaders think those in the pews shouldn't give. "Most of those leaders would probably say, 'you really ought to tithe, but the term 'requires' gets at a theological point," he said.

"Most Christians would say the laws of the Old Testament are not what save you – you're supposed to be giving out of a spirit of freedom, not because you're bound to laws," he said. The National Association of Evangelicals' survey found that 95% of evangelical leaders say they give at least 10% of their salaries to church." (Dan Gilgoff 2012).

According to this study, and many others like it, there has been a shift in the way the majority of Christians view tithing. Most see it as legalistic and demanding; therefore, they don't feel obligated to do it. Still there are some who understand it as an eternal principle established by God in the word of God. Unfortunately, those who understand and incorporate the tithe in their lifestyle are in the minority, and a significant amount of those who say they believe in tithing don't do so faithfully.

One reason there is so much controversy concerning the tithe is because it has been connected to the law more than any other offering. Many people say they don't tithe because tithing is under the law. The word tithe literally means "the tenth." When tithing is mentioned, there is no doubt about the amount one is expected to give. Because of this fact, many say tithing is legalistic and no longer applies to believers today.

The term legalistic implies there is a law determining and enforcing a commandment or ordinance. The question to be answered in the minds of many believers is whether tithing is under the law or exists outside the law.

One of the principles used to interpret scripture is the principle of first mention:

> The law of first mention may be said to be the principle that requires one to go to that portion of the Scriptures where a doctrine is mentioned for the first time and to study the first occurrence of the same to get the fundamental inherent meaning of that doctrine. When we thus see the first appearance, which is usually in the simplest form, we can then examine the doctrine in other portions of the Word that were given later. We shall see that the fundamental concept in the first occurrence remains dominant as a rule, and colors all later additions to that doctrine. In view of this fact, it becomes imperative that we understand the law of first mention. (Cooper D. 1947)

Using the technique given by Dr. Cooper, one can examine the concept of tithing to see if it fits within the confines of law or exists in a realm beyond the reach of the law as an eternal principle of the word of God.

The first mention of the word tithe in the King James Version of the Holy Bible is found in the book of Genesis:

> And blessed be the most high God, which hath delivered thine enemies into thy hand. And he gave him tithes of all Genesis 14:20

There are some interesting lessons to be gleaned from studying this scripture. The first thing is that Abraham was blessed by Melchisedec. In response to this blessing, Abraham gives Melchisedec a tithe of one-tenth of all the spoils he had. I'm not aware of any law instructing anyone to give a specific amount to anyone else during this time. There was no organized priesthood at this time, nor was the Mosaic Law established. What, then was Abraham sowing into, and who was Melchisedec to receive tithes from Abraham?

> "[Gr. *Melchisedek*, from the Hebrew meaning "King of righteousness (Gesenius)] was King of Salem (Gen. xiv, 18-20) who, on Abraham's return with the booty taken from the four kings, "bringing forth bread and wine, for he was the priest of the most high God, blessed him", and received from him "the tithes of all" (v. 20). Josephus, with many others, identifies Salem with Jerusalem, and adds that Melchisedech "supplied Abram's army in a hospitable manner, and gave them provisions in abundance. . .and when Abram gave him the tenth part of his prey, he accepted the gift" (Ant., I, x, 2). Cheyne says "it is a plausible conjecture that he is a

purely fictitious personage" (Encyc. Bib., s.v.), which "plausible conjecture" Kaufmann, however, rightly condemns (Jew. Encyc., s.v.). The Rabbins identified Melchisedech with Sem, son of Noah, rather for polemic than historic reasons, since they wished to set themselves against what is said of him as a type of Christ "without father, without mother, without genealogy" (Hebrews 7:3). In the Epistle to the Hebrews the typical character of Melchisedech and its Messianic import are fully explained. Christ is "a priest forever according to the order of Melchisedech" (Hebrews 7:6; Psalm 109:4); "a high priest forever", etc (Hebrews 6:20), i.e. order or manner (Gesenius), not after the manner of Aaron. The Apostle develops his teaching in Hebrews 7: Melchisedech was a type by reason

- of his twofold dignity as priest and king,
- by reason of his name, "king of justice",
- by reason of the city over which he ruled, "King of Salem, that is, king of peace" (v. 2), and also
- because he "without father without mother, without genealogy, having neither beginning of days nor end of life, but likened unto the Son of God, continueth a priest forever." (v. 3).

The silence of Scripture about the facts of Melchisedech's birth and death was part of the divine plan to make him prefigure more strikingly the mysteries of Christ's generation, the eternity of His priesthood. Abraham, patriarch and father of nations, paid tithes to Melchisedech and received his blessing. This was all the more remarkable since the priest-king was a stranger, to whom he was not bound to pay tithes, as were the children of Israel to the priests of the Aaronic line. Abraham, therefore, and Levi "in the loins of his father" (Heb. vii, 9), by acknowledging his superiority as a type of Christ (for personally he was not greater than Abraham), thereby confessed the excellence of Christ's priesthood. Neither can it be fairly objected that Christ was in the loins of Abraham as Levi was, and paid tithes to Melchisedech; for, though descended from Abraham, he had no human father, but was conceived by the Holy Ghost. In the history of Melchisedech St. Paul says nothing about the bread and wine which the "priest of the most High" offered, and on account of which his name is placed in the Canon of the Mass. The scope of the Apostle accounts for this; for he wishes to show that the priesthood of Christ was in dignity and duration superior to that of Aaron, and therefore, since it is not what Melchisedech offered, but rather the other circumstances of his priesthood which belonged to the theme, they alone are mentioned." (Tierney J. 1911)

The exchange between Abraham and Melchisedec in Genesis 14 establishes an important principle. Abraham's tithes to Melchisedec sow into a priesthood predating the law, the book of Hebrews refers to as an eternal priesthood (Hebrews 7:3) This makes tithing an eternal principle which should be as much a part of modern worship as the freewill offering.

One important thing to note is no one forced or coerced Abraham to offer a tenth to Melchisedec. Abraham freely gave a tithe of all he had gained. In doing so, Abraham incorporated an eternal principle into his finances. Abraham, as a man of great wealth, would have understood this principle better than most. Those who struggle the most with tithing usually struggle with their personal finances as well. Tithing is a kingdom principle expected of citizens of the Kingdom.

When Abraham gave tithes to Melchisedec, he acknowledged Melchisedec as King and Priest. In this scripture, you have the rare opportunity to see the tithe for what it is. Tithing isn't just about giving money; it's a spiritual principle. When you understand that spiritual principles govern kingdom finances, you understand its importance in the life of Christians.

Since Abraham was a strong believer in tithing, it is natural to assume he would have instilled these same principles in the lives of his offspring. As you study the book of Genesis, you will find one of his descendants speaking of tithes as he makes a vow to God. Although Jacob is considered crafty and manipulative, he still demonstrates a strong desire for spiritual things. One might disagree with his methods, but Jacob always found a way to obtain spiritual blessings.

> And Jacob vowed a vow, saying, If God will be with me, and will keep me in this way that I go, and will give me bread to eat, and raiment to put on, So that I come again to my father's house in peace; then shall the LORD be my God: And this stone, which I have set for a pillar, shall be God's house: and of all that thou shalt give me I will surely give the tenth unto thee. Genesis 28:20-22

Here Jacob is attempting to bargain with God concerning the tithe while also attempting to make a covenant with Him. Jacob is saying, in effect, "if you will take care of me, I will give you a tithe of all I get." Now, everyone knows the tithe is not a bargaining tool. It's a principle that works with or without your consent. The interesting thing here is Jacob choosing to offer the tithe to God. This suggests Jacob had been taught about tithing. He understood tithing as a part of spiritual protocol. Jacob knew tithing was the right thing to do, but consistent with his nature, he only wanted to do it if he could be assured there was something in it for himself. Many believers today take a similar attitude. They want to tithe, but only if they have God's assurance they will be blessed for doing so. For those who would argue this is not the tithe, how else would you explain the fact Jacob offered ten percent? This is not an arbitrary figure. It's the same amount Abraham gave Melchisedec.

Today's believer doesn't have to operate like Jacob. You don't need to be further convinced tithing is required. To borrow a saying from Nike, "just do it." You believe your sins are forgiven because the Bible says it. You believe God is a healer because the Bible says it. The same Bible says, "bring all the tithes into my house (Malachi 3:10)." Why is this so hard to believe? The answer is obvious. It doesn't cost you anything to believe your sins are forgiven or that God is a healer. That's all on God, and you get the benefit. Giving tithes would cost you money that you could use for your own benefit. To the carnal mind, this isn't an attractive proposition.

Tithing as a concept and practice predates the law of Moses. It is not bound by the law, nor is it mentioned in the ten commandments. However, there are several times in Levitical law where the tithe is mentioned. Tithes were not the only offerings mentioned by Moses. The laws concerning giving were all instituted to support the priesthood. All the offerings were given by the people to that end. Therefore, tithes, like the freewill offering, must be given freely.

Another reason people say the tithe is intrinsically connected to the law is a strong rebuke mentioned in the Bible concerning the tithe found in the Old Testament book of Malachi:

> Will a man rob God? Yet ye have robbed me. But ye say, Wherein have we robbed thee? In tithes and offerings. Malachi 3:8

Tithes and offerings are mentioned in most sermons preached on this passage, and this scripture is frequently referenced to rebuke the non-tithe payers. This line of thought is reinforced in the tenth verse:

> Bring ye all the tithes into the storehouse, that there may be meat in mine house, and prove me now herewith, saith the LORD of hosts, if I will not open you the windows of heaven, and pour you out a blessing, that there shall not be room enough to receive it. Malachi 3:10

By the time the average preacher reaches this verse, the non-tither has little choice but to repent or accept he is living under a curse.

A more thorough examination of this popular passage from Malachi reveals interesting truths as well as promises often missed when ministers shy away from the topic of tithing. Let's begin our examination of this passage with verse eight and nine:

> Will a man rob God? Yet ye have robbed me. But ye say, Wherein have we robbed thee? In tithes and offerings. Ye *are* cursed with a curse: for ye have

robbed me, *even* this whole nation. Malachi 3:8-9.

This passage begins with a question. Questions allow the reader to draw his or her own conclusions. This question seems rhetorical as it is posed. It's followed by a question which highlights its rhetorical nature: how did we rob God? The answer given brings the question out of the rhetorical arena and into the realm of religion. Now the reader is forced to come to terms with the knowledge their actions are contrary to the word of God.

It's the ninth verse, however, which brings the most backlash from the religious community. As far as the context of the Old Testament is concerned it doesn't seem out of place. There are several places in the Old Testament where curses are mentioned. The problem arises when you take this scripture out of the Old Testament and attempt to apply it to New Testament believers. This presents a moral dilemma to those trying to encourage people to tithe and present biblical evidence to support their position. On one hand, the threat of the curse seems sufficient to discourage the faithful from withholding their tithes; on the other, you have the finished works of Calvary abolish the power of the curse.

The principle of first mentions can help you better understand the concept of the curse. The first time the word "curse" is mentioned in the Bible is in the third chapter of Genesis:

> And the LORD God said unto the serpent, Because thou hast done this, thou *art* cursed above all cattle, and above every beast of the field; upon thy belly shalt thou go, and dust shalt thou eat all the days of thy life: Genesis 3:15

The curse is pronounced not upon man, but upon the serpent behind the transgression. There is no curse pronounced directly upon man.

Now, let's examine what God says to Adam regarding this transgression:

> And unto Adam he said, Because thou hast hearkened unto the voice of thy wife, and hast eaten of the tree, of which I commanded thee, saying, Thou shalt not eat of it: cursed *is* the ground for thy sake; in sorrow shalt thou eat *of* it all the days of thy life; thorns also and thistles shall it bring forth to thee; and thou shalt eat the herb of the field; in the sweat of thy face shalt thou eat bread, till thou return unto the ground; for out of it wast thou taken: for dust thou *art*, and unto dust shalt thou return." Genesis 3:17-20.

God tells Adam the ground will be cursed for his actions. Notice God does not curse Adam here. When God created Adam and Eve, he blessed them. What God blesses cannot be cursed (Numbers 22:12). Instead, the Lord curses the ground. Now Adam's efforts to grow food will be strenuous. The thorns and thistles represent the effects of the curse. Because of the curse, it will be easier to get the things he doesn't want (thorns and thistles) than the things he works for.

This scripture establishes an amazing truth: what God blesses cannot be cursed. Therefore, when you read the third chapter of Malachi, understand man is not cursed for not paying his tithes. When the scripture says "he is cursed with a curse," it is referring to operating under the original curse spoken against the efforts of man. The tithe was instituted to liberate man's effort from the effects of the curse (vs 11). Let's continue studying what scripture reveals about the act of tithing in the third chapter of Malachi:

> Bring ye all the tithes into the storehouse, that there may be meat in mine house, and prove me now herewith, saith the LORD of hosts, if I will not open you the windows of heaven, and pour you out a blessing, that *there shall* not *be room* enough *to receive it.*" Malachi 3:10.

The most important reason given for tithing is found in the beginning of this verse. The people are instructed to tithe so there may be "meat in my house." There needed to be meat in God's house to serve two purposes. First as provision for the priests. The tribe of Levi wasn't given an inheritance among the tribes of Israel. Its needs were provided for by the people through tithes. Second, the meat in God's house provided for the widows, strangers, and others in need.

The house of God was always meant to be a storehouse. This was not so the priest could store up wealth for themselves, but so that there would always be resources to be distributed in the community. In the book of Acts, whenever a believer sold a possession, they would take whatever they got and lay it at the apostle's feet. In turn, the apostles would take what was given and distribute it among the poor and widows. None lacked anything because they had all things in common. This, more than any of the promises that follow, is why the Israelites were encouraged to tithe.

Verse ten and following also highlight the blessings of tithing. The idea of blessings and curses is consistent with the nature of God. These options suggest man has a choice. As a sentient being, man was created with choice. Blessings or curses result from the choices man makes. Although man is not cursed, his choices can lead him into cursed conditions.

The first blessing mentioned in this verse is the blessing of an open heaven. The writer of the book of Malachi is drawing from another Old Testament scripture.

> The LORD shall open unto thee his good treasure, the heaven to give the rain unto thy land in his season, and to bless all the work of thine hand: and thou shalt lend unto many nations, and thou shalt not borrow." Deuteronomy 28:12

In this verse, man's efforts are blessed because of his obedience. The heavens are open to pour out God's best.

The blessing of an open heaven speaks of a mind open and receptive to new ideas and in tune with the plan for man to prosper.

> Beloved, I wish above all things that thou mayest prosper and be in health, even as thy soul prospereth. 3 John 1:2

God's plan for man is to prosper all his efforts. This is not a law, but the will of God. When man is walking in obedience to God's will, he is in tune with God's prosperity plan. The prosperous program God created for man includes tithing. Tithing is not a law restricting God's blessings, but a key that unlocks blessings in the life of the believer.

Connected to the promise of an open heaven is blessing you won't have room enough to receive. The open heaven gives you access to the blessings available to believers. If I were to ask you the difference between you and Bill Gates, the most obvious answer is money. Bill Gates didn't find money that was unavailable to the rest of the world; he found *access* to riches beyond most people's wildest dreams through innovation and ingenuity. In the same way, the open windows of heaven give you access. They allow blessings to be poured into your life. In this same verse, God issues a challenge: prove Me now.

Again, this alludes to man's ability to choose. Deuteronomy 28:23 shows the results of man's disobedience in the form of a curse:

> And thy heaven that *is* over thy head shall be brass,
> and the earth that *is* under thee *shall be* iron.

These conditions make it difficult to demonstrate the blessings of God. Therefore, God says prove Me. You have a choice in how you want to live. So far, no one who has taken God up on this challenge has proved Him wrong. God is always faithful to His word.

Let's continue with verse 11 of Malachi 3:

> And I will rebuke the devourer for your sakes, and
> he shall not destroy the fruits of your ground;
> neither shall your vine cast her fruit before the time
> in the field, saith the Lord of hosts.

The curse mentioned in this verse is part of the original curse. There is no additional curse for not tithing, but when one tithes, his resources are liberated from the effects of the original curse. The devourer is the enforcer of the curse spoken in the garden. He was given legal authority because of sin to destroy the fruits of the ground. Now we see a promise from God concerning the tithe stating the believer who tithes will not suffer the effects of the devourer. The tithe represents sanctification. By offering the tenth, he is sanctifying the ninety percent remaining and liberating his gains from the effects of the curse. To be sanctified means to be set apart. The devourer is denied access to the gains of the believer who tithes faithfully.

Not only is the devourer prohibited from destroying the fruit of the tither's labor, but the tither is given the assurance his crop will not cast fruit before the proper time. Every crop has a time and season when it is ripe. To come up before this time could prove as disastrous as not coming up at all. If you were to plant a crop to come up in late spring and it matured too early, it could be destroyed by frost. In the same manner, there are some spiritual blessings waiting for you to become mature enough to handle them. If they come too early, you might squander them on things you don't need. God knows what you can handle in the season you are in.

Finally, let's turn our attention to verse 12:

> And all nations shall call you blessed: for ye shall be a delightsome land, saith the LORD of hosts.

Ultimately, God wants everyone to see the blessings of the Lord in your life. When you're living under an open heaven, it should be evident in every area of your life. Your life and the lives of those spiritually connected to you ought to reflect the blessings of the Lord.

The tithe only represents ten percent. As a New Testament believer, your offering starts at the tithe. Even in the Old Testament the offerings didn't end with the tithe. This is not to be the end of your offering, but the beginning.

There will always be those who would rather believe tithing is an outdated requirement of the law, than give the Lord a tenth of what He has freely given them. However, paying tithes is not a legal issue, but a trust issue. Either you trust and believe God at His word or you don't. If you trust Him, then you'll have no problem paying tithe.

Here's another way to look at the trust issue. Who are you

most likely to trust: someone you don't know well or someone you have a relationship with and spend time with on a regular basis? Most people would say someone they have a relationship with. Trust is built on and reinforced by relationship. Those who don't trust God with their tithe probably haven't developed a relationship with Him that engenders trust.

Some believe in tithing but feel they can't afford to tithe. These people are bound by a spirit of fear which won't allow them to do what they know is right. If your life is so controlled by fear you can't do what you know is right according to the word of God, then you need deliverance.

Tithing is not God's way of making you behave. Tithing is God's way of demonstrating to others the goodness of the Lord in the lives of believers.

Those who want to tithe will, and those who don't will not. God loves you enough to allow you the freedom to choose. Eternal principles work whether you incorporate them into your life or not. The laws of physics do not need your permission to work. They work because that's how God created this world. You don't have to respect these natural laws as you navigate through life, but life goes a lot smoother when you do. It's the same way with eternal principles. Nobody has the right to demand that you tithe or give at all, but. I've found life tends to go more smoothly when we follow God's principle of tithing.

Real Sacrifices

The first sacrifice noted in the Bible was made by God himself.

> Unto Adam also and to his wife did the LORD God make coats of skins, and clothed them. Genesis 3:21

God sacrificed a kid to provide a covering for Adam and Eve as they were being expelled from the garden. This covering was a type of better things to come. We know that without bloodshed there can be no forgiveness of sins (Hebrews 9:22). Even in his backslidden condition, man still found grace in the eyes of God. By sacrificing an innocent animal, God provided a covering for Adam and Eve's nakedness. From studying this scripture, you will see two things. First, the grace of God to cover man in his fallen condition. Secondly, God making provisions when man cannot provide for himself.

Scripture reveals that everything belongs to God. "The earth is the LORD's, and the fulness thereof; the world, and they that dwell therein." (Psalms 24:1). Since God has created all things, it is obvious that all things belong to him. So why is it even necessary for man to give anything to God? There is only one reason why you would give anything to God. When you give, it is the only tangible way of acknowledging the fact all things come from God.

To understand the true meaning of sacrifice you must look beyond the object being offered and consider other cost. When you do this, you take into consideration other relevant things like time. Most people think their time belongs to them, and it's their choice to decide what is their most important use of their time. Since you are only allotted a certain amount of time, you must prefix your activities in a certain order of importance. In other words, if something is extremely important, you put it at the top of your list of priorities. If something is of less importance you move it further down on the list, and so on. However, if something is not important to your own agenda, and yet it is important to someone or something that you have great respect for and want to honor, then you will sacrifice your agenda and place those things on a higher priority than your own desires.

For your offering to be considered a sacrifice, there must be a cost attached that is above and beyond that which is required by the law or any tradition of man. This is a cost that you must embrace and choose to pay with your own free will. In the story of Cain and Abel it is obvious Cain's offering involved no real sacrifice. Unlike Abel, who brought the firstfruits of his flock, Cain gave what he felt like giving when he felt like giving it. He didn't sacrifice extra time or effort in his offering to God. He did it like it was a responsibility he took no delight in fulfilling. It is impossible to please God with a sacrifice that costs you nothing. To truly understand the meaning of sacrifice you must realize there is a cost.

David realized this more than most people. Let's look at what he did when he was given an opportunity to offer a sacrifice that could have cost him nothing.

> And Araunah said, Wherefore is my lord the king come to his servant? And David said, To buy the threshing floor of thee, to build an altar unto the LORD, that the plague may be stayed from the people. And Araunah said unto David, Let my lord the king take and offer up what seemeth good unto him: behold, here be oxen for burnt sacrifice, and threshing instruments and other instruments of the oxen for wood. All these things did Araunah, as a king, give unto the king. And Araunah said unto the king, The LORD thy God accept thee. And the king said unto Araunah, Nay; but I will surely buy it of thee at a price: neither will I offer burnt offerings unto the LORD my God of that which doth cost me nothing. So David bought the threshingfloor and the oxen for fifty shekels of silver. And David built there an altar unto the LORD, and offered burnt offerings and peace offerings. So the LORD was intreated for the land, and the plague was stayed from Israel. II Samuel 24:21-25

In the story above, David is dealing with the consequences of a foolish decision, and now he finds himself in quite a dilemma. Satan had tempted him to number the children of Israel and he took it upon himself to conduct a census of his army to see how many men were at his disposal. On the surface this might look like a light thing but in the eyesight of God it was a big deal. The reason why this census was so offensive to God was that it was grounded and rooted in pride. David wanted to conduct this census so that he could know how many men he had if he ever decided to go to battle. Even when he went to the captain of his host with this proposition he tried to talk David out of it, but he wouldn't listen to him.

The Bible lets us know that Satan was the source of this idea that had penetrated the mind of David, yet once he began to meditate on it, he became fixated with this census and would not be deterred. So, the Captain of the host and his men went on to number the men of Israel. When they brought the information to David he was confronted by the Prophet Gad. Gad gave David three equally unappealing choices. He could flee from his enemies three months; suffer seven years of famine or three days of pestilence. David chose three days of pestilence. When David saw the Angel of the Lord that was destroying the people he began to intercede to the Lord on their behalf. That is when the Prophet Gad came to him and instructed him to build an altar unto the Lord. David wanted to spare no expenses on this altar. This illustrates a truly repentant heart. The thing that was most important to him was making things right with the Lord. He not only wanted to do this for his own sake but for the sake of the people that were suffering under this judgment.

At this point, David goes to a man by the name of Araunah. He is seeking to buy his threshing floor to build an altar. Being King he could have demanded it be given to him or got it at an outrageously low price. Every citizen of the kingdom is being affected by this plague, including Araunah. Araunah would have gladly consented to any conditions set forth by the king. He evens offers the threshing floor and animals for the sacrifice at no cost to David. This would have been a proposition too hard to resist for some, but David could not accept it. David understood sacrifice at its purest meaning. Sacrifice isn't sacrifice when it doesn't cost you anything. Considering the severity of the offense and the judgment handed down, it would not even be a consideration.

This was not the time to take the things of God lightly, there never is a time to take the things of God lightly.

One of the biggest mistakes you can make as a child of God is to belittle the things that are precious to Him. That is the mistake that Belshazzar the king makes in the 5th chapter of the book of Daniel. While he was feasting and making merry, he commanded the vessels from the Lord's house to be brought to him so he could drink out of them and celebrate. Judgment came to him that very hour because he thought he could take the things of God lightly. God is to be honored in everything we do, especially in our sacrifice.

According to the word of God, all sacrifices in the Old Testament pointed to a better sacrifice only Christ could make (Hebrews 9:13-10:18). In His sacrifice, the requirements of the law are made clearer in application as well as interpretation. All the supporting scriptures point to the same thing; the ultimate sacrifice made by Christ at Calvary. The lessons learned from His example of a dedicated life of obedience and service shows what sacrifice is all about. When it comes to the offering, whatever you sacrifice is not sufficient to repay His sacrifice for all of us.

By now you may be asking yourself what sacrifice means to you as a believer today. The Bible is clear on this point also. In times past, they would sacrifice their time and resources to honor God, but believers today are expected to go further with their sacrifices. Just as the offering was increased beyond the legal limitations of the tithe, so is your sacrifice. The burnt offering of animals is not sufficient for atonement. Jesus has already presented his body for your sin, and you are to present your body for his service.

> I beseech you therefore, brethren, by the mercies of God, that ye present your bodies a living sacrifice,

> holy, acceptable unto God, which is your reasonable service. Romans 12:1

The point of this verse is highlighted by the last two words "reasonable service". The sacrifice God expects is not to give more time or money, but to give your all. When you present your body as a living sacrifice, you are saying all you have belongs to God. This is the ultimate sacrifice a man can make, and yet it is referred to as your reasonable service. Even when you give God your all, you are not doing anything exceptional. The amount you give is not what determines the sacrifice you offer. The sacrifice was made when you presented your body. At that point, it was no longer your money, time, or possessions; it all belonged to God. This is the only real sacrifice. Nothing else is sufficient.

It is liberating to understand this concept. It frees you from your possessions. When your possessions possess you, there's a need for deliverance. It is only by acknowledging that you and all you possess belongs to God that you are truly free. You are not only free to enjoy what God has freely given you, but you are also free to give to others. Knowing God is your source, you can share what He has given you with others with the assurance He will continue to bless you. There is no more giving your last, because even if you don't have anything else in your possession, you know more is on the way.

Giving your whole paycheck as an offering might still feel like a sacrifice, but it's only a sacrifice to the part of you that still believes it's your check and your money. This mindset is extremely difficult to break because you work for your money and feel it really is yours, but when you start to treat it like it truly belongs to God and he has chosen you as a steward, your obedience will put you in position to enter the flow of blessings that has always been God's plan for your life. This is not to imply that you need to give God your whole paycheck, but if you ever feel led by God to make such a sacrifice your obedience is crucial.

These concepts surrounding giving might challenge you to your core. It is only to the amount you are willing to be challenged that you can be liberated. When the disciples were in the midst of a storm, they saw Jesus walking on the water. They all saw him, yet only Peter saw it for what it was. It was a challenge not only to witness Jesus' act of faith but to join Him. Don't be too hard on yourself when you stumble or fail to take the first big step. Sacrifice isn't easy; neither is walking on water. Remember there were twelve on the boat, yet only Peter got out, and he nearly drowned.

If the concept of sacrifice is too much to handle at this point, there are other ways you can honor God with your finances. This leads to the final concept to be discussed concerning giving, that of first fruits.

First Things First

The offering that honors God the most is the first fruit. The first fruit offering is not an easy concept to understand because there is no concrete definition given as to what it means other than putting God first. Everything in the kingdom of God has a divine order. In all things God has the preeminence (Colossians 1:16-18). Still the questions remain; how this is done, and where is the biblical evidence to support it. When a concept is not clearly explained in the Bible, you must try to find its meaning by association and interpretation. By that I mean one may be able to better understand scripture by associating it with the preceding and following scripture. Sometimes this process can help you to better understand the flow of information and continuance of a line of thought. The idea of interpretation can be used by comparing scripture in one verse of text to the same or similar scripture in another verse of text. This is especially true when the verses are connected. By using these techniques as well as other tools available to the Bible Scholar one can gain a better understanding of the concept of first fruit which is mentioned throughout the Bible.

The following scripture offers significant insight into the concept of first fruit.

> Honour the LORD with thy substance, and with the firstfruits of all thine increase: Proverbs 3:9

This scripture refers to a concept of giving known as "first fruit offering." There are several key words you need to examine in this scripture to understand this concept better. The first word you need to examine is "honour". The word translated as honour comes from the Hebrew term "Kabad." It means to be heavy, be weighty, be grievous, be hard, be rich, be honourable, be glorious, be burdensome, be honoured (H 3513). The implication is it isn't easy to honor someone. It can be a burden, which implies it may cost you more than the object you are offering if your sacrifice is to honor God.

Another interesting thing about the word Kabad is it's the same Hebrew word often used for glory. Often when the glory showed up in the Old Testament, the people couldn't even stand because it implies the weighty presence of God. When you honor God, you are inviting His glory. This is the thing one cannot forget. First fruits offerings are meant to be hard because they bear the weight of the glory of God's awesome presence.

Before going any further, you must understand how important it is for one to honor God, because if honoring God causes the glory of God to manifest, then dishonoring God will cause it to depart. When the first fruit is offered willingly to God and received with honor, the glory remains. The first fruit offering was not to be taken lightly and was to be done only in a way that gave glory and honor to God. Notice the scripture did not say give your first fruits or pay first fruits. It said, honour the Lord with your firstfruits. Scripture is very specific about honoring the Lord. This is what makes this offering so special. Although all offerings should honor God, the first fruit offering puts God first, which is the place of honor.

In the book of I Samuel you can see the results of people who chose not to honour God.

> Wherefore the LORD God of Israel saith, I said indeed *that* thy house, and the house of thy father, should walk before me for ever: but now the LORD saith, Be it far from me; for them that honour me I will honour, and they that despise me shall be lightly esteemed. I Samuel 2:31

In First Samuel chapter 2, God sent a stern warning to those who chose not to honor Him. Eli and his sons chose to disregard this warning and continue in their shameful ways. When the ark was taken, it was symbolic of the glory departing. The ark represented the presence and the glory of God. God allowed it to be taken, because His glory cannot remain where He is not honored. Because the sons of Eli chose not to honor the Lord, Israel suffered a mighty setback at the hands of the enemy. Both of Eli's sons were killed in battle and when their father heard the news that the ark of the covenant was taken he fell off the wall and broke his neck.

> And his daughter in law, Phinehas' wife, was with child, *near* to be delivered: and when she heard the tidings that the ark of God was taken, and that her father in law and her husband were dead, she bowed herself and travailed; for her pains came upon her. And about the time of her death the women that stood by her said unto her, Fear not; for thou hast born a son. But she answered not, neither did she regard *it*. And she named the child I-chabod, saying, The glory is departed from Israel: because the ark of

God was taken, and because of her father in law and her husband. And she said, The glory is departed from Israel: for the ark of God is taken. I Samuel 4:19-22

Phineas' wife dies in childbirth, but before her passing she names her son Ichabod. This is a prophetic act on her behalf because the name Ichabod means the glory has departed. The ark represented the glory of God. Its presence is why Israel could never be defeated in battle. When God is glorified, He will make your enemies your foot stool. When God is dishonored, His presence cannot be a part of your defeat. Rather than remain with them in dishonor and defeat, because of their failure to honour God, He allowed the ark to be taken by the enemy.

Another word you should examine is substance. This word comes from the Hebrew term "Hown". It means wealth, riches, substance (H 1952). In the economy of God, how you honor God becomes a wealth management tool. Your substance is not what sustains you; God sustains you. Your substance is to be used for God's glory. With that being the case, then whatever you acquire in this lifetime should be used for His glory and to honor Him. As you continue to honor God, He continues to bless you. This is how you enter the flow of supernatural blessings.

Let's look at the word firstfruits. This word comes from the Hebrew term *"re'shiyth"*. This means first, beginning, best, chief (H7225). Now you see why it can be so challenging to offer to the Lord the firstfruits. This word literally means you give the best you have to the Lord. It embellishes the true meaning of the word sacrifice. So, when you offer your first fruit, it means you are offering the best that you have. It should be noted that this is the result of an offering that honors God. This is not something that should be done arbitrarily, but prayerfully when one is led by the Holy Spirit.

Now I want to bring your attention to the verse immediately following this scripture. "So shall thy barns be filled with plenty, and thy presses shall burst out with new wine." (Proverbs 3:10). As you can see this verse is a continuation of the preceding one. Not only do they follow each other in chronological order in the scripture, they also reinforce each other. When you put these scriptures together, you can see a good example of the principle of association I mentioned earlier. Together these verses bring out one of the eternal principles of the word of God: **the principle of seedtime and harvest** as it is set forth in the Bible. What is said in verse nine refers to the seed being sowed. Verse ten refers to the harvest one will reap. Your obedience to the first fruit principle is the seed sown in verse nine, and your barn being filled with plenty is the harvest you will reap from this simple act of obedience.

> And there came a man from Baal-shalisha, and brought the man of God bread of the firstfruits, twenty loaves of barley, and full ears of corn in the husk thereof. And he said, Give unto the people, that they may eat. And his servitor said, What, should I set this before an hundred men? He said again, Give the people, that they may eat: for thus saith the LORD, They shall eat, and shall leave *thereof*. So he set *it* before them, and they did eat, and left *thereof*, according to the word of the LORD. II Kings 4:42-44

This miracle began with a first fruit offering. Because someone chose to honor the Lord with their first fruit, an opportunity was made available for a miracle. Notice that the man brought the first fruit to the house of the prophet. This was done without provocation or coercion. It was offered in the form of a seed. Because of the anointing on the life of the prophet, this first fruit offering was subject to supernatural increase. Although still in line with seedtime and harvest, the harvest was increased supernaturally. That is why it is important to offer the first fruit with honor, because this allows God to add super to your natural. I will deal with the eternal principle of seedtime and harvest more in depth in the next chapter; for now, it is important to understand this first fruit offering was presented as a seed.

In Deuteronomy chapter twenty-six, the people are instructed to bring an offering of the first fruit unto the Lord. Upon releasing their offering, they are also instructed to affirm that the Lord brought them into a land flowing with milk and honey. While offering the first fruits, they recited their history--how they were taken out of Syria and spent time in captivity in Egypt. They confessed that the Lord delivered them. The first fruit offering presented them with an opportunity to rehearse in the ears of the priest all the good things the Lord had done for them.

Not many ministries receive the first fruit offering these days. Those that do usually receive it at the first of the year. A ministry that teaches the concept of first fruit will have the opportunity to experience firsthand the financial as well as spiritual benefits of first fruit offering. This practice serves as a reminder to the congregation to put God first in all things. The first fruit offering is a good opportunity for one to remind themselves of the goodness of the Lord. It is presented as an offering of thanksgiving for the blessing one has received from the hand of the Lord. The ministries that I am familiar with that still receives the first fruit offering, are some of the most blessed ministries that I have had the pleasure of witnessing. The most important aspect of the first fruit offering is that it serves as a reminder to the congregation that God has the preeminence in all things.

Seedtime and Harvest

> While the earth remaineth, seedtime and harvest, and cold and heat, and summer and winter, and day and night shall not cease. Genesis 8:22

This scripture is given by God as a promise to the inhabitants of the earth. It is also the first mention of seedtime and harvest in the Bible. This promise is not given specifically to believers. It expresses a universal principle which God said will remain while the earth remains. Let's examine how this principle connects to the New Testament concept of sowing and reaping.

God spoke of seed in the beginning of creation:

> And God said, Let the earth bring forth grass, the herb yielding **seed**, and the fruit tree yielding fruit after his kind, whose **seed** is in itself, upon the earth: and it was so. Genesis 1:11 [emphasis added]

Although seedtime and harvest are not mentioned together in this verse, the implication is seed is given for the sake of reproduction. Without seed there can be no harvest. This was God's idea from the beginning. In fact, God always uses seed in his generational plan. In the garden after the fall of man, God promised the seed of the woman would bring redemption (Gen. 3:15).

The principle of seedtime and harvest is an eternal one which transcends time. As you study this principle, you will find that promises made in one generation can come to pass in another generation. Even acts that occur before the birth of a child are still credited to the unborn child, as is evidenced by the following scripture.

> And as I may so say, Levi also, who receiveth tithes, payed tithes in Abraham. For he was yet in the loins of his father, when Melchisedec met him. Hebrews 7:9-10

This scripture highlights the generational nature of seedtime and harvest. Abraham was the great grandfather of Levi, yet Abraham was referred to as Levi's father. Even though Levi wasn't born, he was credited with paying tithes in the loins of Abraham. That seed gave his natural descendants the right to receive a harvest of tithes paid to the Levitical priesthood. Because the principle is eternal, even those who would sit in the office of the priest after the Levitical priesthood was abandoned would still be entitled to receive tithe as a harvest of the seed sown. All believers are blessed along with faithful Abraham because he sowed into an endless priesthood, utilizing an eternal principle.

Although seedtime and harvest operate in the spiritual realm as well as the natural, there are still some important differences that must be acknowledged. In the natural realm, seedtime and harvest are cyclical events. Therefore, it is easy to predict when the season is changing. You can tell by ques from nature when the seasons are preparing to change. As fall approaches the leaves begin to change colors and fall from the trees. This is a sign to farmers that their harvest will soon be coming. In the spiritual realm, changes in seasons are not governed by the calendar, or naturally recurring cyclical events. The one constant being that seedtime always comes before harvest. Although God changes times and seasons, it is impossible to get a harvest before a seed is sown.

Just as there is a time and a season for natural things, there is also a time and a season for spiritual things. Spiritual seasons are not as easy to predict as natural ones, but there was a tribe in the Old Testament that had an uncanny knack for discerning times and seasons.

> And of the children of Issachar, which were men that had understanding of the times, to know what Israel ought to do; the heads of them were two hundred; and all their brethren were at their commandment. I Chronicles 12:32

These men had a supernatural ability to discern times and seasons. They were always consulted before Israel made important decisions. Just as a farmer would know when it was the best time to plant a crop, they would know the best time for Israel to make choices that would determine the destiny of the nation. They gained this knowledge because they understood seasons.

Even if you were like the children of Issachar and could discern seasons and predict when your spiritual harvest would come, this information would be useless if you hadn't sown any seed. To reap, you must sow. This principle is as true in the spiritual as it is in the natural. These two forces are inseparable.

The prophet Amos made an amazing prophecy regarding seedtime and harvest that I believe applies to the times in which we live.

> Behold, the days come, saith the LORD, that the plowman shall overtake the reaper, and the treader of grapes him that soweth seed; and the mountains shall drop sweet wine, and all the hills shall melt.
> Amos 9:13

God is telling His people by the mouth of the prophet that He is going to speed up seedtime and harvest, so the people of God will receive an instant harvest. I believe that in the times we live in, you can realize a harvest as soon as you sow the seed. Therefore, it is important during this dispensation to take advantage of every opportunity to sow seed in good ground.

It is important to understand that God is talking about spiritual seed. Although the manifestation will show up in the natural realm, they still must be in line with the eternal principles of seedtime and harvest. Spiritually, God can speed up your harvest and give you instant increase. Instant harvest is not without precedent. When Jesus received the seed of the bread and loaves, He lifted it up to heaven and blessed it. He instantly received a harvest large enough to feed five thousand. This prophetic act was a preview of what would be available to believers today.

Multiplying the fishes and loaves is one of the greatest miracles recorded in the Bible. It represents a miracle of divine provision. But after careful review of the miracle you will see it all began with a seed. The fishes and loaves were the seed sown. Jesus didn't produce the food from thin air. This would've been a violation of His own divine principle.

Miracles are not magic; they are the result of the principle of seedtime and harvest. Most miracles recorded in the Bible began with a seed. At the wedding when the water was turned into wine, the water was the seed. When the widow in the Second Kings 4 had a debt she couldn't pay, the prophet requested a seed. All she had was a cruse of oil. The seed was multiplied instantly, and she paid her debt with enough money left over to live on. The woman with the issue of blood had a seed of faith, and it generated the miracle she so desperately needed. Remember, Jesus said greater works shall you do also. If you put yesterday's miracles in today's perspective, you will see this is already happening. It is ludicrous to believe Jesus could multiply bread and fish yet be unable to multiply your money. Those who can receive this shall see instant harvest in their finances in the season in which we live.

Although the concept of seedtime and harvest can be sped up to the point of instant harvest, there are principles concerning seedtime and harvest which cannot be violated under any circumstances. Even miracles defying natural circumstances are still subject to natural seasons established by God.

> And he said, About this season, according to the time of life, thou shalt embrace a son. And she said, Nay, my lord, thou man of God, do not lie unto thine handmaid. And the woman conceived, and bare a son at that season that Elisha had said unto her, according to the time of life. II Kings 4:16-17

Although the Lord did a miracle in the life of this woman who had been barren, it was still done in accordance to the laws of nature. She was told she would embrace a son, but it would be according to the season. In other words, she would have to carry the baby for nine months just like every other woman. When Mary had Jesus, it was by immaculate conception, but she still had to carry Him until the season He was due.

When you understand the true nature of seedtime and harvest, you understand the reason why you should always be willing to sow a seed. You are only increasing your harvest. A harvest is only possible when seed has been sown. Too many people expect the word of God to provide some sort of shortcut where God does everything for them and they just reap the benefits. That is not how grace operates. Grace can multiply your seed beyond your wildest expectations, but you still need to sow the seed. Seedtime and harvest is a principle that God will not violate to accommodate your doctrine. It was true in the Old Testament and it was true in the New Testament, and it is just as true today.

This idea is highlighted by the apostle Paul:

> If we have sown unto you spiritual things, *is it* a great thing if we shall reap your carnal things? I Corinthians 9:11.

The idea of sowing and reaping is an eternal principle predating any man-made laws.

Sowing and reaping would be more easily understood by agrarian societies of the middle east. Unlike the hunter gatherer societies that developed in Europe, their lifestyle revolved around a cycle of seedtime and harvest. This concept could be easily assimilated into their worship. They intrinsically understood that reaping was a direct result of sowing. When the seeds were sown, or planted thy were still responsible for watering, and removing weeds. The real work that brought about the harvest happened underground in the unseen realm. They were forced to trust as much in what was not seen as they did in what was seen.

All these seeds were different. Some produced crops quicker than others. Some were more plentiful than others. Some flourished in different seasons than others. No matter what the seed was, or the process required for a harvest, one aspect remained constant: to reap a harvest, one had to plant a seed. There is no way around this simple concept.

> But this I say, He which soweth sparingly shall reap also sparingly; and he which soweth bountifully shall reap also bountifully. II Corinthians 9:6

To someone who made a living off the land, this concept would be self-explanatory. No one had to force the farmer to sow, if he wanted to reap he had to sow. Because this concept is so powerful and effective, one should sow in expectation rather than fear. We no longer live in agrarian societies, and this may be the reason believers are not so quick to grasp the meaning of this scripture.

In the next verse, Paul goes on to connect sowing and reaping to the condition of the heart. Paul reminds the offeror what one receives is directly connected to what one gives:

> Every man according as he purposeth in his heart, so let him give; not grudgingly, or of necessity: for God loveth a cheerful giver (v. 7)

Don't miss the spiritual implications of this verse. Not only are you sowing money or material things, but also a state of mind. Sowing out of necessity only increases your need but sowing cheerfully increases your joy.

Some will never know the joy to be gained from giving. Yet there are others who seems to get an extra boost from giving. Many people are happy to receive, but those who have learned the joy of giving are happiest when they give. These people will never have to be coerced or convinced to give. On the contrary, they seek out opportunities to give. They have truly learned the meaning of the scripture "it is more blessed to give than to receive."

If you really want your joy to increase, have joy when you give. The next opportunity you have, try giving cheerfully. It might not be easy at first, but when you begin to reap the benefits you will discover it's the only way to give.

Because seedtime and harvest are eternal principles, God will initiate them. Therefore, it is God's responsibility to provide seed to the sower.

> Now he that ministereth seed to the sower both minister bread for your food, and multiply your seed sown, and increase the fruits of your righteousness.
> II Corinthians 9:10

This verse reinforces the fact all things come from God, who not only gives you the seed, but also guarantees your increase. God does not multiply the same as we do. He said in His word one can cause a thousand and two can cause ten thousand of the alien armies to flee. Our job is to sow the seed God gives us.

The key to understanding this scripture is discerning the differences in seed and bread. That which is seed is given to your care to be sown, and bread is provided for your natural needs. One of the things that hurts believers more than anything else is not discerning when God has given them seed. If there is a need for ministry and you have asked God to meet that need, sometimes God answers by providing seed. This seed, when sown, will produce a harvest, including provision for the needs of the ministry.

The believer who mistakenly assumes everything that comes his or her way is for their own consumption will never know the benefits associated with the concept of seedtime and harvest. This is the reason why prayer is so important to the people of God. Through prayer God can reveal to you the spiritual applications of the principle of seedtime and harvest. This spiritual principle is as sure as gravity, so be careful how and what you sow.

> Be not deceived; God is not mocked: for whatsoever a man soweth, that shall he also reap. Galatians 6:7

Giving must be directed by purpose. It is not wishful thinking or something to be manipulated by gimmicks. You must prayerfully purpose what you are determined to give and offer it cheerfully. This should be done knowing not only will you reap what you sow, but also how you sow. Paul doesn't want to mislead the believer, but to instruct him on the seriousness of this act. He instructs the believer to give bountifully, because he knows they will reap not only what they have sown, but also as they have sown. To expect otherwise is to mock God in disobedience to his eternal principles. Seedtime and harvest is the key to supernatural abundance. It is evidenced throughout the Bible. It is just as true today as it was in Biblical times. While the earth remains you still have time to enter the supernatural flow of blessings by utilizing this eternal principle.

The Principles of Stewardship

It is never too early to teach stewardship to a child. Some learn stewardship when they get their first pet. They are taught they not only have a pet, but they have the responsibility of another life in their hands. Because in most cases this is something that they have asked for, it makes it easier for them to be held accountable for the animal's upkeep. If stewardship is taught in the right manner, he or she will accept it and see it as a rite of passage to even greater responsibility. This is the lesson your heavenly father desires to teach you concerning stewardship.

A common mistake people make when teaching on stewardship is equating everything concerning stewardship to money. Money is an excellent example of stewardship because it can be easily quantified. You can give numerical value to the benefit as well as the cost. Not only does money have measurable value, it is also universally accepted as a means of exchange. Everyone can relate to monetary issues. However, if you are to live a successful Christian life, you must be a good steward over all your resources.

As valuable as money is, there is another resource everyone shares that is also measurable and universally accepted. This resource can be traded for its determined monetary value. Although it is exchanged for and is measured in units that facilitate this exchange, there is one important quality that makes it immeasurably different from money. This resource cannot be replenished. When it is gone it is truly gone. In case you haven't figured it out, I am talking about time.

Except for your soul, time is perhaps the most valuable resource you have. Most people don't view time this way. They waste so much of the time they have. Many people live their lives as though they are never going to die. Still there is a limit to the time available to fulfill their desires and reach their goals. Time is inextricably connected to every resource you have. It doesn't matter how much money you have if you run out of time to use it for God's purposes. It doesn't matter how large of a ministry you have and how many people you are serving if you run out of time to serve them. Norman Vincent Peale once stated that the graveyard has the greatest collection of unused potential in the world. It is filled with doctors who never picked up a scalpel and architects who never designed a house. There are countless athletes, singers and business men and women who never took the time to perfect their craft. Often the person who succeeds in life is the person who realized the value of his or her time.

Jesus told Peter "And I will give unto thee the keys of the kingdom of heaven: and whatsoever thou shalt bind on earth shall be bound in heaven: and whatsoever thou shalt loose on earth shall be loosed in heaven." (Matthew 16:19). Jesus was letting Peter know when his plans and desires were aligned with Heaven, and he did his part in the physical realm, his efforts would be supported by spiritual principles. This is the way stewardship works. If adhered to, what originates in the spiritual realm will be manifested in the physical realm.

When you adhere to stewardship principles in the earth realm, you are releasing (loosing) your finances on earth, and in effect they are released (loosed) in Heaven. When you resist the principle of stewardship, you find your finances are bound in Heaven. In other words, there is no super added to your natural. It is like jogging with weights on your ankles. There is already the force of gravity that is keeping you bound to the earth and the extra weight only increases that force. Occasionally God will allow a word to come your way that will cause you to remove the weight and enjoy the added freedom of his blessings on your life.

The same principles that apply to spiritual things also apply to natural things. A good way to understand this is by observing the concept of gravity. According to science, gravity operates both in space and on earth. Although it is the same force, its power is diminished the farther away you get from the earth. This is supported by the fact that a rocket uses up to ninety percent of its fuel trying to escape the earth's gravitational force. However, when the rocket leaves the earth's orbit the pull of gravity is considerably less. Like gravity, the closer a spiritual principle is to where you live, the more difficult it is to apply.

The concept is easy to grasp in theory, but its application is much more challenging. As you begin to incorporate these principles into your life, you are immediately impacted by the force of old habits and ways of operating. Like gravity these forces are attempting to keep you bound to old ways of operating that are not in sync with kingdom principles. As you continue to incorporate kingdom principles you begin to feel the weight of the world's system releasing you into the flow of God's kingdom.

Jesus often used parables to demonstrate kingdom principles to his disciples. While teaching his disciples about stewardship he chose the parable of the talents. There are many rich lessons to be learned from this parable. Jesus uses it to help his disciples understand the need for good stewardship. Within this parable is a wealth of information that demonstrates the benefits of good stewardship as well as the perils of unfaithful stewardship.

> For the kingdom of heaven is as a man travelling into a far country, who called his own servants, and delivered unto them his goods. And unto one he gave five talents, to another two, and to another one; to every man according to his several ability; and straightway took his journey. Then he that had received the five talents went and traded with the same, and made them other five talents. And likewise he that had received two, he also gained other two. But he that had received one went and digged in the earth, and hid his lord's money.
> After a long time the lord of those servants cometh, and reckoneth with them. And so he that had received five talents came and brought other five talents, saying, Lord, thou deliveredst unto me five talents: behold, I have gained beside them five talents more. His lord said unto him, Well done, thou good and faithful servant: thou hast been faithful over a few things, I will make thee ruler over many things: enter thou into the joy of thy lord. He also that had received two talents came and said, Lord, thou deliveredst unto me two talents: behold, I have gained two other talents beside them. His lord said unto him, Well done, good and faithful servant; thou hast been faithful over a few things, I will make

thee ruler over many things: enter thou into the joy of thy lord.

Then he which had received the one talent came and said, Lord, I knew thee that thou art an hard man, reaping where thou hast not sown, and gathering where thou hast not strawed: And I was afraid, and went and hid thy talent in the earth: lo, there thou hast that is thine. His lord answered and said unto him, Thou wicked and slothful servant, thou knewest that I reap where I sowed not, and gather where I have not strawed: Thou oughtest therefore to have put my money to the exchangers, and then at my coming I should have received mine own with usury. Take therefore the talent from him, and give it unto him which hath ten talents. For unto every one that hath shall be given, and he shall have abundance: but from him that hath not shall be taken away even that which he hath. Matthew 25:14-29

This passage of scripture is often misunderstood by beginning Bible readers. Even some preachers use this as an illustration of what happens to people who don't use their God given talents wisely. Careful study of the word of God reveals not only the meaning of the parable but also the content of the parable itself. Since it is often referred to as the Parable of the Talents, it is important to define the word "talent" as it is used in this passage. The word translated as talent comes from the Greek word "talanton". The meaning used in this passage of scripture is "a sum of money weighing a talent and varying in different states and according to the changes in the laws regulating currency (G5007)." A silver talent represents 100 lbs or 45 kgs of silver, and a gold talent is about 200 lbs or 91kgs of gold. Although the Bible does not specify which metal was used, either one would represent a considerable amount of money during those times.

This parable, like so many others that teach stewardship or other aspects of the economy of God, operates on the same basic principles discussed in the previous chapters. Again, you see the principle of seedtime and harvest, or sowing and reaping. Before going on a long journey, the master sows into their lives by giving them talents. These talents were an investment he made into their stewardship. This is seedtime. As you know, there is always a period of time between seedtime and harvest. Even in the natural during seedtime, seed is put into the ground and nobody is expecting a harvest at that time. During this time of gestation within the earth, someone must make sure the seed receives the proper amount of sunlight, water and fertilization. If this is done properly, a good harvest will be the result. The essence of stewardship is assuming full responsibility for what someone has entrusted to your care.

The first principle of stewardship is **one must first recognize the value of what one is entrusted with to become a better steward.** Once you recognize the value of any resource, you become a better steward of that resource. The man, who recognizes the value of his time will live his life like he knows it's valuable. He must be a good steward of his time because he knows he can never get it back. A person who understands the value of money will make their choices with greater deliberation because they realize that although it can be replenished, this resource is still limited.

Each servant was given a different amount of money to manage. Since these were servants that were already under his authority, it is obvious the master knew who could be trusted with each amount. He would not have given his servant more than he could handle, nor too little to sufficiently exhibit his capabilities. In fact, the scripture says they were each given an amount according to their abilities. Each one was expected to gain a return in proportion to what he was given. With this being the case, no one should have come up short.

The second principle of stewardship is as follows. **No man can be held accountable for more than he is given.** All stewards are asked to give an account, but no one is asked to give an account for another man's goods. You can see this principle in process by what happened to the first two servants. Each of them doubled what was given them. The lord didn't expect the servant with two talents to come up with five more, nor the servant with five to come up with only two more. The last servant received only one talent The Bible does not say they were given any specific instructions; however, based on the actions of the first two servants, it can be inferred they were expected to manage what they were given in a profitable way.

After entrusting each steward with a predetermined amount of money the Lord goes on a long journey. There is no way of knowing how long this journey was or how far he went, but from the text you can deduce he was gone long enough to provide ample time for them to have profited in whatever endeavor they had chosen. This brings us to the third principle of stewardship. **Stewardship is most accurately measured when the steward is left alone with whatever is entrusted to him without close monitoring or support.** It is considerably easier to manage someone's affairs when they are there to advise you, steer you through pitfalls and traps, and constantly monitor your activities. You could lean on them for information invaluable to your stewardship. The only problem is this would not be real stewardship.

While you are training or in an apprenticeship, you will have someone with you to answer your questions and assist you with difficult situations. The time will eventually come when you will be left alone. This is when you must be able to summon all the skills you acquired while training to perform the job. This is when stewardship will be tested on the proving ground of performance. It is like when a teacher gives a test to a pupil. During class time he can ask as many questions as he wants. If he is not sure of a concept, he can even stop the teacher by raising his hand and asking for clarification. Once the test begins, however, the teacher is no longer available to answer questions or give instruction. This is the time when you learn whether or not you gained the necessary skills and abilities to do what you have been taught to do. Real stewardship begins when you are alone and must make independent decisions with far-reaching consequences.

The fourth principle of stewardship is **true stewardship can only be gauged by the steward's ability to faithfully increase what he has been given.** A good and faithful steward is one that can take whatever he or she is given and find ways to increase it. **Faithfulness and increase** are the most important gauges to determine the effectiveness of one's ability as a steward. It is much easier to find someone to maintain what you have than it is to find someone who will find ways to increase it. In doing so one must take what is not theirs and treat it like it was theirs when it comes to finding profitable ways to increase the value. To do this one must be a shrewd trader and honest enough to take what he has been trusted with and increase and turn it all over to his master without taking some for himself. This type of service illustrates not only one's ability to manage the affairs of others, but also his willingness to do it honestly and profitably. This is described in the Bible as the highest quality a steward can have.

> Moreover it is required in stewards, that a man be found faithful. I Corinthians 4:2

This scripture highlights the most important quality expected in any steward. The word moreover is taken from the Greek word "loipon". This word means remaining, the rest, hereafter and for the future. (G3063). The implied meaning seems to be that when considering a steward to serve you, the most important quality that one should seek is faithfulness. The word faithful found here comes from the Greek word "Pistos". This word means a person who shows themselves faithful in the transaction of business. (G4103). In this case faithfulness is not just a matter of you showing up or being on time but it also encompasses your activities while present. This means that a person can show up to work every day on time and still not be a faithful employee. Therefore, your faithfulness as a steward is directly linked to your ability to increase whatever you have been entrusted with.

The law of faithfulness and increase does not stop with your duties as a steward. This law is also exemplified by the Lord of the house when he comes from his journey. This law is not limited to rewards. Each of the successful stewards receives a reward for their service. Not only are they given more responsibility, but also, they are given ownership. When you are an owner you are held responsible for all aspects of ownership. By adhering to all the laws of stewardship these faithful stewards could be elevated to the position of owners.

They shared in the labor and they were also able to share in the reward and the joy of the Lord.

So far, I have only talked about the good stewards who were able to apply the principles of stewardship effectively and in doing so honored their Lord. Now let us examine the final servant who chose another route. It is obvious by his words that he does not understand the principles of stewardship.

The first principle of stewardship is that one must understand the value of what one is being entrusted with. By hiding his talent, he shows that he understands that it is valuable enough not to lose, but it also illustrates the fact that he does not appreciate the value of the opportunity that is being offered to him. So many times, people are slothful in their stewardship positions because they fail to see the opportunity that is placed before them.

The third principle of stewardship states that stewardship is most accurately measured when the steward is left alone with whatever is entrusted to him without close monitoring or support. He also failed to acknowledge this important principle. When he is left alone, he is left to make some important decisions that can go either way. This means he can take risk with what he is entrusted with. This does not imply he should take foolish chances with his Lord's money, but he has the leverage to make informed decisions just as he would with his own money. He was not given an exuberant amount of money so even if he lost some of it he could still say he took a calculated risk and things did not turn out right. All investments involve a certain amount of risk, and usually the greater the risk the greater the return. The same opportunities that were available to the two servants who doubled their investments were available to him.

Then there is the fourth and final principle of stewardship, which states that true stewardship can only be gauged by the steward's ability to faithfully increase what he has been given. This unfaithful steward did not respect this law either. As a good steward his focus would not be on keeping what was entrusted to him, but on increasing what he was given. On the surface, it might seem as though he was really concerned about his lord's goods, but upon deeper observation he was simply being lazy. It was a lot easier to bury the talent and present it to his master when he came back than to put forth the effort necessary to gain more.

Increase doesn't come without a price. This is in all realms whether you are talking spiritual or natural the law works the same. When a child is born he or she might only weigh between 6 and 8 pounds, and measure between 19 and 21 inches long. This same child when he or she is grown can weigh over 200 pounds and stand over 6 feet tall. This increase did not come out of thin air. The child grew because someone faithfully fed it until it could feed itself. Although it is designed to grow, it could not grow without effort, either its own or someone else's.

Whether gifts of the Spirit, or the anointing of God, one must mature in whatever their calling or gifting entails. In his second epistle, Peter wrote the words "grow in grace." Although to each is given a measure of faith, it is the responsibility of each believer to increase that measure as needed to benefit the kingdom of God. The natural realm works almost exclusively on the law of increase. It is the same in the spiritual realm. Yet this servant did not see the need to increase what he was given. Instead he thought it would be good enough just to present his master with what was given to him.

This unwise servant is forced to deal with consequences that he does not anticipate because as a steward he chose to ignore spiritual principles. When his master returns he presents to him the talent that he was given. Then he proceeds to make excuses as to why he did not do what was expected of him. He falsely accuses his master of reaping where he had not sown and picking up where he had not laid down. It is obvious he has misjudged his master because the master sowed into all of their lives by giving them talents to exercise their stewardship. Because he failed to see the value of the opportunity given him, he did not put into operation the first principle of stewardship, or any of the subsequent principles.

This servant's attitude represents that of someone who never expects to be successful in life. He saw his master as unjust and greedy. His worldview seems to be shaped by fear and apprehension. He worked for the same man and had the same opportunities as the other servants, yet he found a way to fail when the others found ways to succeed. It is possible the master's knowledge of his servant's disposition is why he only entrusted this servant with one talent. It is so easy to blame others for the things you don't have, but at some point, you must take inventory of yourself and realize you have also had opportunities you squandered. During a lifetime, many people have had ideas and opportunities fall into their laps and done nothing with them.

It is sad when you think about the fate of this unfaithful servant when his master returns. He is judged by the very same words he spoke to his master. There is a great lesson to be learned in this parable. Is it possible the Lord is letting you in on a greater secret than surface study of the word can reveal? Maybe it's not just the servant's actions that condemn him. When you reflect on what he told his master, his thought process is revealed. If his words are any indication of his worldview, he saw the world as a hostile environment where no one could benefit unless they broke all the laws of God's economy. If his master was truly like he said then he should have acted accordingly, but his words betrayed his actions. He knew his Lord expected an increase, but he failed to act on the knowledge he had. That is what the Lord told him when he returned. When you have a negative worldview, you can only see ways to fail, and excuses not to succeed. This sort of thinking can only lead to failure and defeat.

God expects his people to be productive in all aspects of their lives. You are to be a city set upon a hill. This doesn't mean you will not encounter setbacks, but you will overcome them. Ultimately you are supposed to live a life that produces fruit in the kingdom of God.

> I am the true vine, and my Father is the husbandman. Every branch in me that beareth not fruit he taketh away: and every *branch* that beareth fruit, he purgeth it, that it may bring forth more fruit.
> John 15:1-2

One of the most painful things you will endure as a Christian is the purging process. This involves cutting away the things that thwart your growth. The reason this is so painful is because it usually involves people or things attached to your life that you aren't ready to let go. People are sometimes not willing to let go of people or things holding them in unproductive patterns of thought or behavior. When those things are removed, you experience new joy and peace. There can be lots of hesitation when it comes to taking this step, but you must be willing to take whatever step is necessary to be a good and faithful steward of kingdom resources.

This is a good place to take an inventory of yourself. Some of the questions you might ask yourself is where am I being unfaithful, or what can I do to become a better steward of the things that the Lord has entrusted to me? We all can do better in every area. The only way to do that is to look inward and demand the change that is needed. One day all of us will have to give an account of our stewardship. I know that I want to hear the words well done. What about you?

The Law of Exchange

Twenty plus years ago while I was living in Savannah, Tennessee, I went through some difficult times. I didn't have a regular job and was trying to make a living washing cars. A revival was going on at the church I was attending, Love Tabernacle Church of God in Christ. The Spirit was moving, and I was enjoying the presence of the Lord. As they raised the offering. they asked everyone to put in twenty dollars. Twenty dollars wasn't a lot of money, but it was all I had at the time. At first, I thought about just giving $5 and saving the rest for supplies to wash more cars. While I was contemplating how much to give, I felt the gentle nudge of the Holy Spirit prompting me to give it all.

The thought of giving it all hit me like a bolt of lightning. Not only was this all the money I had, but my rent was overdue, and I didn't have anything to eat. Sitting in the assembly, I realized the twenty dollars wouldn't be enough to pay my bills. I recalled something I heard a preacher say years before, "if it's not enough to meet your need, then it's enough to sow a seed." In that moment, I decided to give it all.

I didn't realize it at the time, but I wasn't just releasing money; I was also releasing the fear and uncertainty keeping me in bondage. I was initiating the law of exchange. I was exchanging my fear and uncertainty for trust and courage. The next day, one of the deacons from my church came by the house. I hadn't shared my financial situation with him. During his visit, he gave me enough money to pay my rent. A little while later, I was blessed with a job and was able to move into a 3-bedroom home.

The law of exchange is illustrated throughout the Bible. Abraham's interaction with Melchisedec in Genesis chapter fourteen is a clear example of this principle in action.

Melchisedec met Abraham returning from the slaughter of the kings. After greeting Abraham, Melchisedec spoke a blessing over Abraham's life. This ministered to Abraham's spiritual needs. Melchisedec gave Abraham and his men bread and wine, and Abraham gave Melchisedec a tenth of his spoil.

Melchisedec is an Old Testament archetype of Christ. He represented the eternal priesthood established by God. The bread and wine are more than natural provisions; they are also an Old Testament allusion to the communion. While Melchisedec blessed Abraham, Abraham gave tithes of all he had. Not only is Abraham giving tithes before the law, he is tithing in accordance to eternal principles predating the law.

Now let's contrast Abraham's experience with Melchisedec with his encounter with the king of Sodom:

> And the king of Sodom said unto Abram, Give me the persons, and take the goods to thyself. And Abram said to the king of Sodom, I have lift up mine hand unto the LORD, the most high God, the possessor of heaven and earth, That I will not take from a thread even to a shoelatchet, and that I will not take any

> thing that is thine, lest thou shouldest say, I have made Abram rich: Genesis 14:21-23

Abraham realized accepting anything from the king of Sodom would violate an eternal principle of the kingdom of God. The king of Sodom was not in a spiritual position to bless Abraham and was therefore not able to give anything of value to him. Also, Abraham was already in possession of what the King of Sodom was offering. Therefore, the proposition coming from the king of Sodom was completely out of order with kingdom principles and by refusing, Abraham was acknowledging the power of the law of exchange. Because of these principles, Abraham chose not to receive anything from the King of Sodom.

Paul alludes to the law of exchange in his letter to the Corinthian church:

> If we have sown unto you spiritual things, *is it* a great thing if we shall reap your carnal things? I Corinthians 9:11

Paul is emphasizing the exchange which occurs when those who minister to your spiritual needs receive carnal or natural provisions.

The law of exchange simply means something must be given in order to receive. In the natural realm, if one is to make an exchange it is usually for something of equal or at least comparable value. No one likes to come out of a trade with a loss. If one is to take a loss it is usually the one who is able to do so or is unaware that he is losing in the transaction.

In the spiritual realm the greater is willing to take less so that it is accounted as a blessing to someone else. This principle is highlighted by the writer of Hebrews:

> And without all contradiction the less is blessed of the better.
> Hebrews 7:7

This scripture is also referencing Abrahams dealing with Melchisedec. As a priest he is in a spiritual position to impart blessings to Abraham. The blessing he spoke over Abraham's life was far more valuable than the spoil that he shared with him. This entire transaction was in accordance with the law of exchange.

The law of exchange is especially evident in our dealings with God. There is nothing that we can offer God to compensate for all that we receive from God. The following scripture illustrates how much God is willing to give in exchange for so little we give to him.

> To appoint unto them that mourn in Zion, to give unto them beauty for ashes, the oil of joy for mourning, the garment of praise for the spirit of heaviness; that they might be called trees of righteousness, the planting of the LORD, that he might be glorified. Isaiah 61:3

Notice how the law of exchange is expressed over and over in this scripture. When you deal with a Holy and just God, what you receive from Him is always greater than what you give to Him. Yet you must give Him something for there to be an exchange.

God is saying, "if you want beauty, bring Me your ashes." Beauty represents anything coveted by man. Ashes, on the other hand, are what's left when everything of value is burned up. Ashes are usually discarded because they are of no value. This speaks of the transformative power of God. He takes what is discarded or rejected and makes something beautiful with it. It is amazing what God can do with something you see little or no value in. Consider what He did for Moses when Moses faced Pharaoh.

> And the LORD said unto Moses and unto Aaron, Take to you handfuls of ashes of the furnace, and let Moses sprinkle it toward the heaven in the sight of Pharaoh. And it shall become small dust in all the land of Egypt, and shall be a boil breaking forth with blains upon man, and upon beast, throughout all the land of Egypt. And they took ashes of the furnace, and stood before Pharaoh; and Moses sprinkled it up toward heaven; and it became a boil breaking forth with blains upon man, and upon beast. Exodus 9:8-10

God instructs Moses to lift ashes that are of no value to the children of Israel toward heaven. When Moses lifts the ashes, they are transformed from something useless into something powerful.

The reason the law of exchange is so powerful is because it always works in favor of those who are willing to release. Sometimes people refuse to release things that are no longer of any value. You have no power over the things you hold on to. When you release them, you are empowered in ways you never would have imagined.

Next, he says he will give you the oil of joy for mourning. Oil is symbolic of the anointing. Look at what the word says about joy:

> Thou lovest righteousness, and hatest wickedness: therefore
> God, thy God, hath anointed thee with the oil of gladness above thy fellows. Psalms 45:7

This not only speaks of joy as an anointing, but also a source of promotion. Notice the word says above thy fellows. Most people don't think of joy as a byproduct of the anointing. To receive that anointing of joy one must be willing to release mourning. It is not always an easy transition, but it is one you must be willing to make at some point. In biblical times there was an allotted time for mourning. When kings and judges died the people were usually allotted forty days for mourning.

The book of Ecclesiastes states there is a time for mourning. "a time to weep, and a time to laugh; a time to mourn, and a time to dance;" Ecclesiastes 3:4. Mourning is part of the normal grieving process, however if one continues to mourn excessively one can become obsessed with mourning. If one is not careful he could become so overwhelmed with grief that he is not able to go on with life. Notice that the time of mourning is followed by a time to dance. This alludes to a balanced life. One that is not overcome with grief. "weeping may endure for a night, but joy *cometh* in the morning. Psalms 30:5B. the only solution the word offers for overcoming mourning is joy, and God offers that to us in exchange for mourning.

Finally, the word say that he will give you the garment of praise for the spirit of heaviness. As a child of God, you don't have to live your life underneath a cloud of depression or heaviness. Garments represent clothes or something that can be seen. "Rejoice in the LORD, O ye righteous: *for* praise is comely for the upright." Psalms 33:1. The word comely is derived from the Hebrew word na'veh. It means seemly, comely, or beautiful. Once again you see that what he wants to give you is so much greater than what he is requesting from you. Heaviness or depression does nothing to enhance your appearances, but if you will give it to God he will beautify you with the garments of praise.

Jesus alluded to the law of exchange in His discourse with the woman at the well. This is one of the most beautiful examples of the law of exchange given in the Bible. When Jesus encounters this woman, he asked her to give him something to drink. He did not request water simply because he was thirsty. His request for water opened the door for her to become a participant in the law of exchange.

Instead of complying with this request, the woman begins a discourse on the dealings between Jews and Samaritans. Jesus knew there was discord between these groups; however, He was making a personal request of her which had nothing to do with either group. The law of exchange only concerns the parties in the exchange, even if many others may stand to benefit. Rather than enter a debate with her on the state of relations between the Samaritans and Jews, Jesus' response to her brings the focus back to the exchange He desired to initiate with the woman:

> Jesus answered and said unto her, If thou knewest the gift of God, and who it is that saith to thee, Give me to drink; thou wouldest have asked of him, and he would have given thee living water. John 4:10

When Jesus tells her she could have living water, she realizes she is about to miss out on something essential to her soul. She responds: "give me this water that I thirst no more." At no point does she offer to give Him the water He asked from her. Her response showed that she was not prepared to participate in the law of exchange. She wanted the living water (spiritual) but offered no water (natural) for him to drink.

There can't be an exchange if you are not willing to give something.

In many ways, believers today are like this woman. She wanted something from Jesus but didn't want to give what He required. When it was obvious she wasn't going to comply, Jesus changed the subject. He is always willing to meet us halfway, but we must be willing to at least take a step. It is not always a leap of faith, sometimes it is just a step. The woman at the well never took that step. She received wonderful revelations about her life that were life altering. That was grace but imagine what she might have received if she only gave him a drink of water.

God never asks anything of you unless you're able to give it, and what He desires to give you is always greater. Those who understand the law of exchange are constantly looking for opportunities to give unto the Lord. There is a song that says, "you can't beat God giving." Whoever wrote that song must have had a good understanding of the law of exchange. When you give unto the Lord you always receive more than what you give.

When you participate in the offering at your local church, you have an opportunity to participate in the law of exchange. As you give to the ministry you receive strength, encouragement, and guidance from those the Lord has ordained to minister to your spiritual needs. You might be giving money, but what they provide to you is much more valuable. Your soul is worth more than money or anything else you could give to the man or woman of God. Don't hesitate to give of your finances to the kingdom of God because God is not hesitant to provide the things you need. When this concept is practiced faithfully and prayerfully, you will find it is one of the most awesome principles established in the word of God.

It's one thing to give God ashes or a drink of water when what you give has little or no value to you. But what about when resources are scarce, and you don't feel you can spare what God is requesting? These are the times God is offering you the opportunity to gain the most from the law of exchange. The times you feel God gently tugging on your heartstrings to give more than you feel you can afford to give could be the times the Lord wants to demonstrate the law of exchange in your life.

> So he arose and went to Zarephath. And when he came to the gate of the city, behold, the widow woman was there gathering of sticks: and he called to her, and said, Fetch me, I pray thee, a little water in a vessel, that I may drink. And as she was going to fetch it, he called to her, and said, Bring me, I pray thee, a morsel of bread in thine hand. And she said, As the LORD thy God liveth, I have not a cake, but an handful of meal in a barrel, and a little oil in a cruse: and, behold, I am gathering two sticks, that I may go in and dress it for me and my son, that we may eat it, and die. And Elijah said unto her, Fear not; go and do as thou hast said: but make me thereof a little cake first, and bring it unto me, and after make for thee and for thy son. For thus saith the LORD God of Israel, The barrel of meal shall not waste, neither shall the cruse of oil fail, until the day that the LORD sendeth rain upon the earth. I Kings 17:10-14

This is the law of exchange operating in the spiritual and manifesting in the natural realm. Even though there was a famine, the widow woman in this passage was willing to offer a drink of water to the prophet. But when it came to food, it was a different story. The scarcity of the food affected her hospitality toward the man of God. She informed him things weren't normally this way, but her current circumstances didn't allow her the option of preparing a meal for him. The prophet took her fear and offered his faith. Because of her obedience to the word of God, which could only be done by faith, she receives divine provisions for herself and her son during the famine.

The law of exchange is a spiritual force God uses to change people's circumstances and elevate their faith. When you are dealing with spiritual darkness, you need spiritual help to gain the victory. This woman had been traumatized by the loss of her husband and the impending famine. Faced with so much adversity, the door was open for a spirit of fear to convince her she was facing certain death. The prophet uses the law of exchange to replace her fear and hopelessness with faith and courage.

As she began moving in faith, God takes her little and multiplies it so that not only does she have provisions for the man of God, but for herself and her son also. Her seed was a little cake baked for the prophet. When it was mixed with faith, it multiplied instantly. The harvest from that seed was enough to sustain her and her son for an entire year. That is why she needed spiritual help. Sure, she already had what she needed, but it wasn't enough. When she sowed it into the ministry of the prophet, it was multiplied by the law of exchange.

The law of exchange is seen in operation throughout the Bible, but there is no greater example than Jesus. He took our sin and gave us his life. No one else in history was qualified to make that sacrifice because truly the lesser is blessed of the greater. Even though salvation is freely given, it cost Jesus His life. He who was greater became sin, so that we who are less can live sin free. The stench of our sin was replaced by the sweet aroma of his sacrifice. There is no greater love than this a man will lay down his life for his friends. Because of his great sacrifice we have gained eternal life. He made the sacrifice once and the law of exchange has caused it to multiply until all who call upon the name of the Lord shall be saved.

Money is the Solution

Years ago, God spoke a word to me more powerful than I ever could have imagined. I was ministering at a church in Florida, and a young lady came forward for prayer. While I was ministering to her, the Lord told me to tell her *"money is not the problem. It is the solution."* A short time later, the woman's pastor informed me the woman came into a considerable amount of money. When the woman paid her tithes, it was enough to pay off the mortgage on the church.

As powerful as this testimony is, I didn't realize the power of the words the Lord spoke to me at the time. I spoke in obedience to God, but it would be years before I realized the awesome truth they contained. Sometimes when the Lord gives you a word it is not just for this particular time or person; sometimes, it speaks of eternal truth. This was one the first eternal truths that I received from the Lord. It has never left my spirit. The more I meditated on this truth, the more the Lord revealed to me about it. He began to show me that what I think about money is as important as how I handle money. In fact, it is more important. My thoughts about money not only determine how I handle money, but how much money I have the opportunity to handle.

The first thing I began to examine was my thought life. If I consistently thought of money as a problem, then on some level it would represent something I needed to avoid. People who have a problem with alcohol usually find they handle themselves better if they avoid alcohol. When you have a problem with certain people, you seek to avoid those people. If you see money as the problem, it makes it awfully hard to attract more money into your life. On a conscious level, this might seem like no big deal, but subconsciously there could be a lot more at stake.

This sounds good in theory, but what are some of the practical things you can do to incorporate this truth into your life? There must be a reason why money is always a problem for some while others always seem to have the money they need for whatever project they're working on. Sometimes it becomes necessary to make a conscious decision for your unconscious thought processes to line up with. For example, when attempting to break certain habits, a person will choose not to be around certain people, places, and things that can trigger certain thought processes that lead to undesirable behaviors.

As I began to realize how powerful this truth was, I realized there must be a way to incorporate it into my ministry and life. Since God would never say anything that is not in line with his word, I began to search the Bible for what the word had to say on the subject. As I studied the word, I found a passage of scripture that not only supported what the Lord spoke to me, but put everything into perspective in a way I never noticed before.

> A feast is made for laughter, and wine maketh merry: but money answereth all *things*. Ecclesiastes 10:19

Now see what it says in the ERV edition of the Bible.

> People enjoy eating, and wine makes life happier.
> But money solves a lot of problems.

There it was in the word of God. Money is in fact the solution, but there was so much more to this scripture that was yet to be revealed. Feasting represents the natural things all men need and enjoy. Wine represents the pleasures of life. These are things that bring joy and meaning to life. Although some are not necessities, they still make life more enjoyable.

The key to this scripture is that all the things one desires in life cost money. Everything from the most basic of human needs to the most extravagant of man's desires cost money. Don't get too spiritual here; I'm talking about material things.

In the kingdom of God, all things are subject to kingdom principles, including money. So, if money is not the ruling principle, you are probably wondering what is. The answer is purpose. Purpose guides everything in the kingdom of God. Money and purpose are eternally entangled. When you pursue the purposes of God, money will show up when it is needed. In fact, when you pursue the kingdom, anything you need will show up.

> But seek ye first the kingdom of God, and his
> righteousness; and all these things shall be added
> unto you. Matthew 6:33

To say money is the solution means nothing until you first define the problem. There must be an idea or a clearly defined need. Let's say you want to start a ministry feeding the poor. This is a good idea. You might even be aware of some ministries already providing this service. Here is where you must lay aside your ego and ask the question, "if someone is already doing this, do I need to do it also, or would my efforts be more productive helping them in their ministry?" If you realize your time and resources would be better utilized helping an existing ministry, then your problem is solved. You might be able to accomplish your goals by combining resources with someone else who could use your help.

Now let's say you've considered helping others with food service, and either there is no one you know with a ministry, or they are too far away for you to join forces with them. After you have identified a need in your community, the next thing you need to do is assess that need. You must determine how many people you will be feeding and how much it will cost per person. With this information, you will know how much your costs will increase as the population you serve increases

Once you've determined what your cost will be per person, the next thing you must do is assess your financial situation. If you are in position to offer this service to the community and absorb all the costs yourself, then you're ready to get started serving free meals. Not only will this be a blessing to your community and ministry, but it will also be a seed sown into the lives of others. On the other hand, if you realize you really don't have the resources to devote to feeding others, then you have a problem.

The problem is not money, but a lack of money or other resources to bring your plans to fruition. This isn't merely a play on words; it's clearly defining the problem to find a reasonable solution. At this point you should've already laid out a clear plan of action and have cost in mind. Now is the time to pray and seek God for the means to accomplish His purposes. Prayers with purpose are like the focused light of a laser. These prayers will penetrate heaven. They will shine light on new ideas and expose resources you might never have uncovered if you viewed money as a problem. In fact, God might reveal a solution that doesn't cost you any money. You may learn about grants and/or other unconventional ways to raise money to accomplish the purposes of God. Remember the scripture says money answers all things and solves many problems. The money and resources will come when they are needed. It is up to the Lord how and when they will come.

It is even more rewarding to realize money for God's purposes has always been a part of His plan.

> But thou shalt remember the LORD thy God: for it is he that giveth thee power to get wealth, that he may establish his covenant which he sware unto thy fathers, as it is this day. Deuteronomy 8:18

The Lord has a plan for you to acquire wealth. The wealth you will accumulate has a purpose. God gives you the power to get wealth to "establish his covenant." His covenant includes wealth, health, and prosperity in every area of your life.

Those who seek money without purpose will usually find themselves in need. In the kingdom of God, you don't get money by seeking money. You find money while fulfilling God's purpose. As God reveals His purposes to you, the money you need will show up. Don't waste your time asking God for money unless it is for a specific purpose. This is not to say you shouldn't ask God for money, but you should be specific in your request.

> Ye lust, and have not: ye kill, and desire to have, and cannot obtain: ye fight and war, yet ye have not, because ye ask not. Ye ask, and receive not, because ye ask amiss, that ye may consume *it* upon your lusts. James 4:2-3

Prayer is all about motive. According to James's epistle, asking amiss is equated to not asking. You must learn to be honest with God and yourself. Some people want more money with no idea what they would do with it if they received it. These people can ask, but they will not receive what they're asking for.

If you truly need more money, try this before you pray. Write down all the things you need that you don't have money for at this time. Next, go over your list to make sure you haven't left anything out. This is your list; you don't have to leave anything off because you think it will cost too much. God is not broke. You can't make a list He can't handle. Lastly, write down what you believe these things will cost. Now you have a specific amount you can pray for God to give you. Pray about the list and the amount every day until you can recite it without reading it, then put it away. Don't look at it again for seven years. In those seven years, you will have everything on your list if these are things you need. In most cases, it will take less than seven years. You will be pleasantly surprised when you revisit your list.

As you seek to fulfill the purposes of God, you will find you need more money than you have at times. In these moments, you will see the hand of God making provisions for His purposes. Money was never meant to impede the purposes of God, but to facilitate them. When you see money as the solution, you will realize it has always been a part of God's plan. Like all things, money has a place, and finding its place can be one of the most liberating experiences you could ever have.

A Place for Money

One day while I was at work, one of the pharmacists was explaining to me how his new pastor had changed the order of their service. Instead of receiving an offering during the middle of the service, they started taking theirs at the end of the service. Naturally I thought this would cause the offering to diminish. To my surprise, he said not only did it not decrease, but it increased.

After this discussion, the conversation continued to rehearse itself in my mind. When this happens, I know God is trying to get me to see something I've missed or reveal some spiritual truth to me. It's not always when you are reading the bible or during religious exercises. It was while meditating on this conversation that the Lord spoke this truth into my spirit: *you must learn to put money in its place.* Not long afterwards I changed the order of service at my congregation. We started receiving our church offering at the end of the service instead of in the middle. By doing this I learned some interesting things. Just like at my co-worker's church, I saw our offering increase.

If your church is like most I've been to, the offering is taken just before the word with maybe a song before the pastor gets up to preach. That might be what you're used to, but that is out of order. The word of God should have the preeminence in the worship experience; money should never come before preaching the word. In most churches, praise and worship comes before the word. This doesn't take away from the word; rather, it serves to prepare the atmosphere and the hearts of the people to receive the word of God. When they have received the word, their hearts have been prepared to bless the house that has blessed their souls. This is probably the reason why the offering increases when it is taken up at the end of the service instead of afterwards.

Money has a place in ministry, but you must be led by the Spirit to find it. In this case, it was at the end of the service. It was only after I made this simple change that the Lord began to express to me why this was important. It's not about getting a bigger offering or saving time. There are other, more important concerns. When everything you do is influenced or controlled by money, you lose sight of what's truly important. This is not to imply money doesn't have its place, but to emphasize it must be kept in its place.

There are many people who have not mastered the idea of money. Too many ministries approach money with the wrong attitude, then become upset when money will not behave properly for them.

Whenever you want to do something major what is the first thing that usually comes up? The cost. How much is this going to cost? Cost is the killing field of many great ideas and the burial place where plans are laid to rest.

This is one of those places where there must be a paradigm shift in the kingdom of God. You see, things in the kingdom do not operate like things in the world. In the world, money has the place of preeminence and rules all things. In the kingdom, it is just the opposite. Look at what Jesus said concerning the tithe:

> Woe unto you, scribes and Pharisees, hypocrites! or ye pay tithe of mint and anise and cummin, and have omitted the weightier *matters* of the law, judgment, mercy, and faith: these ought ye to have done, and not to leave the other undone. Matt. 23:23

These men were so consumed with the materialistic aspects of tithing, they forgot there were more important things in the mind of God than money. Jesus wasn't telling them not to tithe or give money, but to put money in its place.

There is a real danger in not respecting the place of money. If you're not careful, you'll become so consumed by the love of money that you'll have little or no regard for the things of God.

> For the love of money is the root of all evil: which while some coveted after, they have erred from the faith, and pierced themselves through with many sorrows. I Tim. 6:10

This scripture does not call money evil. Many people have wrongly reached this conclusion. It is speaking about the love of money that causes men to covet things not ordained for their lives. This love for money can lead to choices that leave you spiritually shipwrecked. The love of money can cause you to lose sight of priorities and make choices based only on financial gain. When that happens, it opens the door to all sorts of spiritual wickedness and hinders the move of God. When man's priorities interfere with God's priorities, man is left to his own devices. That is why so many churches today are spiritually dead. You cannot advance spiritually unless all things are done decently and in order.

During the days of Eli, he allowed his sons to take advantage of the people's offerings. Eli was warned about this. When he failed to heed the warning, Israel was defeated and the ark of the covenant was taken by the Philistines. Israel was not defeated because their army was inferior; they were defeated because the priest allowed their priorities to get out of alignment with the priorities of God.

Just because judgement doesn't come immediately, doesn't mean its not coming. They were given space to repent. Instead they became emboldened and continued in their wicked ways until their disobedience cost them their lives.

You would think the last place you would find this behavior is in the house of God, but it was the same way in Jesus' day:

> And Jesus went into the temple of God, and cast out all them that sold and bought in the temple, and overthrew the tables of the moneychangers, and the seats of them that sold doves, and said unto them, It is written, My house shall be called the house of prayer; but ye have made it a den of thieves. Matt. 21:12-13

When Jesus entered the Temple, He found the house of God completely out of order. Not only were they buying and selling in the house of God, but they were making merchandise of the people of God. If a worshipper entered the temple to offer a sacrifice, the priest would say it was blemished and disqualify it for sacrifice. In some cases, after traveling a long distance to offer the sacrifice, the worshipper had no choice but to buy another animal from the priest, most likely at an exorbitant price.

Just as in the days of Eli, the people were grieved in their worship because they were being taken advantage of by the priest. At this point, the focus of the priest was no longer on God, but on money. When this happens, not only are the people being grieved, but the Holy Spirit is also grieved. This is in direct contrast to the plan and purpose of God.

Notice what Jesus says. Instead of being a house of prayer, the temple had become a den of thieves. This is a direct result of men not putting money in its proper place. Not only are there natural consequences to this behavior, but spiritual consequences that are even more profound.

> And the blind and the lame came to him in the temple; and he healed them. (v. 14)

While the focus is on exploitation and financial gain, there is no mention of healing. The spiritually impotent priests hid behind laws and tradition that did not allow the lame and blind to enter the temple so their powerlessness was not exposed.

The sad part about all this is the same thing is happening today. Men and women of God who have been called to minister to the needs of the people of God are more focused on what they can get *from* the people than what they can get *for* them. When money is put in its place, the ministry will take care of its own needs, and the needs of the people will not be neglected. When greed and selfishness rule the hearts of church leadership, the Holy Spirit is grieved. There is no healing, and there is no deliverance. This is why people are walking into services every Sunday and leaving the same way they came, because the focus is no longer on God but on money.

Although this situation is bad, it is not hopeless. When you remember whose house it is, you realize He will only let this go on for so long:

> thus saith the Lord GOD; Remove the diadem, and take off the crown: this *shall* not *be* the same: exalt *him that is* low, and abase *him that is* high. I will overturn, overturn, overturn, it: and it shall be no *more*, until he come whose right it is; and I will give it *him*. Ezekiel 21:26-27

This scripture speaks of the priesthood being abolished. The diadem and crown were worn by the high priest as a symbol of sovereignty. To remove the diadem meant the priesthood was changing. This is an extension of the prophecy given in I Samuel at the transgressions of Eli's sons. When Jesus came on the scene, He represented a new priesthood that would not be connected to the Levitical lineage. Instead, it would be after the order of Melchizedek.

When the money changer's table was overturned, this was a prophetic act that represented the priesthood being overturned. Notice what God tells the prophet Ezekiel: I will overturn, overturn, overturn. On three different occasions, the Spirit of God would intervene in the affairs of the Temple. The first time was in Eli's day. The second time was in Jesus' day. There remains one more time when everything that *can* be shaken *will* be shaken. I believe that time is the day we live in. Those who are exploiting and making merchandise of the people of God will be exposed for what they are.

During the final time when the priesthood is overturned, you will see things change unlike anything we have ever witnessed. No longer will the people of God be dependent upon ministers who have no regard for the things of God. Business as usual will no longer be tolerated in God's house. Those ministries that have honored God will be honored.

There is a shift coming to the house of God. God is calling ministers who will have a heart for the people of God. These men and women of God will not be consumed by financial gain; they will have a heart that burns for the things of God. Leaders in high places will be exposed for the corruption in their hearts. Entire denominations will suffer a great falling away. Not a falling into sin, but a decrease in membership as men and women everywhere seek a more fulfilling and rewarding relationship with Jesus Christ.

We are living in exciting times, but they are also dangerous times. Ananias and Saphira realized they were living in exciting times, but they failed to realize they were also living in dangerous times. This oversight cost them their lives. The miracles God is about to do in the financial realm, are more important today than ever before, but they are not to be taken lightly. Finances should be approached as prayerfully as anything else in the ministry.

A transfer of wealth is coming to the body of Christ in these last days:

> A good man leaveth an inheritance to his children's children: and the wealth of the sinner is laid up for the just. Proverbs 13:22

This scripture does not mean wealth is being stored up for church folks. It will take more than your name on a roster to qualify for this wealth transfer. This wealth is laid up for the just. Being in church doesn't make you just. It isn't a matter of works. There is only one way to be just, and that is by your faith:

> For therein is the righteousness of God revealed from faith to faith: as it is written, The just shall live by faith." Romans 1:17

If the wealth of the sinners is laid up for the just, and the just shall live by faith, what is that saying to you? This is a good question. The answer has been laid out before you. Every principle outlined in this book requires faith. When you incorporate these principles into your Christian journey, you are walking by faith, and all the promises in God's word belongs to you, including the wealth of the sinners. God bless and prosper you.

Acknowledgements

It's impossible to thank everyone whose mentoring, teaching, and assistance have contributed to this book and my life. The following acknowledgements are my humble attempts to acknowledge those individuals who most expressly made this book a reality.

I would like to thank Erica Hearns of Serious Season Publishing Services for her diligent work bringing this book to life. Thank you for all the sacrifices you made and the countless hours you spent editing, formatting, and preparing this book for publication. I would also like to thank Joleene Naylor for bringing my vision for the cover of this book to life.

Thanks also to Bishop Brandon B. Porter for accepting my request and writing an exceptional foreword for this book. Your words perfectly encapsulate the message and set the readers' expectations for *Under New Management*; Dr. Joseph Fisher and Dr. Barry Chaney, the Co-Founders of Adullam Bible College, for their continued confidence in my abilities to bring forth a timely word from the Lord for our students past, present and future, and; the students of the word of God, at Adullam Bible College and abroad, who will diligently search the scripture to see if these things are so, and apply every morsel of truth to their lives. A thousand times, thank you.

Above all, thanks be to God, who always causes us to triumph.

About the Author

Dr. Edward J. Hearns earned his Bachelor of Science in University Studies from the University of Tennessee at Martin. He also earned Bachelors, Masters, and Doctorate degrees from the Midwest College of Theology. Dr. Hearns serves as the pastor of the Friendly Church of God in Christ (COGIC) in McKenzie, Tennessee. He is also the President and Co-Founder of Adullam Bible College in Gainesville, Florida. Dr. Hearns' other publications include *No Lack, Cracking the Relationship Code, The Road to Azusa, and Concerning Spiritual Gifts.*